ISSUES OF BUDDHISM

Joe Walker

Hodder Gibson

A MEMBER OF THE HODDER HEADLINE GROUP

The Publishers would like to thank the following for permission to reproduce copyright material:

Photo credits
Title page © Oliver Burston/Debut Art; page 2 (top) © Karen Kelly/Fotolibra, (bottom) © Alex Todd/Fotolibra; page 5 © Moksajyoti/Clear Vision Trust; page 9 (left) © P. Manner/zefa/Corbis, (middle) © Bettmann/Corbis, (right) © Rune Hellestad/Corbis; page 10 (left) © Homer Sykes/Alamy, (middle) © A Gosh/Israel Sun/Rex Features, (right) © Lachetka/Rex Features; page 17 © Maciej Wojtkowiak/Alamy; page 25 © Maciej Wojtkowiak/Alamy; page 29 © Crack Palinggi/Reuters/Corbis; page 57 © Ann Ronan/HIP/Scala, Florence; page 75 © Pornchai Kittiwongsakul/AFP/Getty Images; page 91 (top) © Ciby 2000/Recorded Picture Co/The Kobal Collection/Blanshard, Richard, (middle) © Roman Soumar/Corbis, (bottom) © World Religions/Christine Osborne; page 92 © www.TopFoto.co.uk; page 93 © V&A Images/Alamy; page 94 (top) © Kevin Lang/Alamy, (middle) © Alison Wright/Corbis, (bottom left) © Joanna Bilska/Alamy, (bottom right) © Chris Lisle/Corbis; page 95 (top) © Michele Burgess/ Superstock, (bottom) ©Tony O'Brien/The Image Works/TopFoto; page 96 © Free Agents Limited/Corbis; page 97 © Maciej Wojtkowiak/Alamy; page 99 © Roman Soumar/Corbis; page 109 © Fredrik Renander/Alamy; page 111 © chinch gryniewicz/World Religions Photo Library; page 112 © Jim Young/Reuters/Corbis; page 113 © World Religions Photo Library/Christine Osborne; page 131 © Cancan Chu/Getty Images; page 137 © Circa Religion Photo Library/William Holtby; page 139 © Jeremy Horner/Corbis; page 144 (top) © World Religions Photo Library/Alamy, (middle) © Circa Religion Photo Library/Bip Mistry, (bottom) © Circa Religion Photo Library/William Holtby; page 148 © Ei Katsumata/Alamy; page 150 © Chad Ehlers/Alamy; page 151 © Chris Lisle/Corbis.

Acknowledgements
The author would like to thank Dharmacarini Anagarika Kalyanavaca, Director of the Edinburgh Buddhist Centre for her helpful comments on the manuscript and Jill Proctor of the RE Department at Portobello High School. Also, thanks to Lorna and David again for their limitless patience and understanding.

Every effort has been made to trace all copyright holders, but if any have been inadvertently overlooked the Publishers will be pleased to make the necessary arrangements at the first opportunity.

Although every effort has been made to ensure that website addresses are correct at time of going to press, Hodder Gibson cannot be held responsible for the content of any website mentioned in this book. It is sometimes possible to find a relocated web page by typing in the address of the home page for a website in the URL window of your browser.

Hodder Headline's policy is to use papers that are natural, renewable and recyclable products and made from wood grown in sustainable forests. The logging and manufacturing processes are expected to conform to the environmental regulations of the country of origin.

Orders: please contact Bookpoint Ltd, 130 Milton Park, Abingdon, Oxon OX14 4SB. Telephone: (44) 01235 827720. Fax: (44) 01235 400454. Lines are open 9.00 – 5.00, Monday to Saturday, with a 24-hour message answering service. Visit our website at www.hoddereducation.co.uk. Hodder Gibson can be contacted direct on: Tel: 0141 848 1609; Fax: 0141 889 6315; email: hoddergibson@hodder.co.uk

© Joe Walker 2006
First published in 2006 by
Hodder Gibson, an imprint of Hodder Education,
a member of the Hodder Headline Group
2a Christie Street
Paisley PA1 1NB

Impression number   5 4 3 2 1
Year   2010 2009 2008 2007 2006

Cover photo by Oliver Burston/Debut Art
Cartoons © Moira Munro 2006. Illustrations by Jeff Edwards and Fakenham Photosetting
Typeset in Garamond 12.5/14.5pt by Fakenham Photosetting
Printed and bound in Great Britain by Martins The Printers, Berwick-upon-Tweed

A catalogue record for this title is available from the British Library

ISBN-10: 0340 915 854
ISBN-13: 978 0340 915 851

Contents

Contents

Introduction

Buddhism in RMPS

Look around the shops in most major cities in Scotland and you will find Buddha statues, paintings, incense sticks. Sometimes these are curiously mixed in with healing crystals, and all sorts of new age stuff. People de-stress themselves by going to meditation classes. Are these kinds of things linked to Buddhism? Sometimes yes, sometimes no. You should have done some basic studying of Buddhism by now – who was the Buddha, what is meditation, and so on. Maybe your RMPS teacher has had you 'meditating' in class... Now that you're at Intermediate or Higher level we want you to take the next step. This book aims to get you thinking about what's behind it all. What do Buddhists believe? What is their philosophy? Do they have a theology?

This book, like the others in the series, also aims to get you thinking. The course is structured to have you thinking about what we call the Human Condition, the Goals of life, and how we achieve these goals – the Means. Buddhism offers a perspective on these issues which has similarities to and differences from other religions. This book is designed to challenge you, not just fill you full of facts about Buddhism. As often as possible, the aim is for you to think about your own response to what Buddhists believe and so help you to think more clearly about your own beliefs. It should also help you pass your exam, but that's just one step along the way. The book is designed to get you thinking about the big questions of life and the big issues by challenging you with Buddhist beliefs about these issues.

The book has different ways of trying to get you thinking:

Text: Explanatory information about the issues, presented in an easy-to-read way, which covers important facts, as well as prompting reflections and questions about the information given.

Talking Points: Learn by talking to each other and finding out your different beliefs. Talking through the issues will also help you to make greater sense of them.

Time Outs: This gets you to slow down and take time to reflect on what you're learning or to do something to find out more. Sometimes you need to take more time to think things through more carefully.

You won't learn everything about Buddhism in this book. It matches up with curriculum requirements for this level. There's a lot of material about Buddhism out there and more views about it than you can imagine. Hopefully this book will be a helpful starting point.

Thank you for using the book, and in the words of Buddhism, may all beings be happy!

Joe Walker

History; Spread; Variety; Healthcheck

What is a World Religion?

There has been much discussion about whether Buddhism counts as a religion or not. This is probably because many people feel that you need a belief in the existence of a God for it to be a religion and Buddhism doesn't have that. Others say that you need to communicate with a divine figure through something like prayer and Buddhists don't do that either (some think it's ok, others frown on it). So, is Buddhism a religion? There is no clear answer to this question, however, Buddhism is included in RMPS, so perhaps we don't need to worry about this right now.

A World Religion is a faith which you'll find all over the world. Buddhism is much more obvious in some countries than others, but then so are all world religions. How do you know if someone is a Buddhist? If your neighbour shaves his head and walks around in orange robes and sandals, then it's obvious that something 'different' is going on. However, people don't have to dress in any particular way to be a Buddhist, nor do they ever have to carry out Buddhist devotions anywhere else but at home. They don't have to join with any other Buddhists or set up temples, so maybe your neighbour is a Buddhist after all!

Scotland has a healthy Buddhist population. There are Buddhist temples – sometimes they are in converted houses and sometimes they are specially built grand places like Samye Ling in Eskdalemuir. The Friends of the Western Buddhist Order is an organisation for Buddhists, and joining the Order is a clear expression that you have engaged with the Buddhist faith. Even here, though, there are various 'levels' of being a Buddhist, from the newly interested to the ordained. You can become a Buddhist monk in Scotland, or you can just follow the faith in your own way. For many people, this flexibility is one of the attractions of Buddhism. Buddhism is (partly) about finding you own way towards a better understanding of life, using the teachings of the Buddha to guide you. In fact, Buddhism isn't always called Buddhism. Some Buddhists simply call it the Buddha Dhamma – the way (or teaching) of the Buddha. Buddhists also vary in their beliefs and practices. There are 'schools' and 'sects' in Buddhism as in other religions. Not all Buddhists know all the information or theory you'll study in this book. They might consider putting some of it into practice more important. You might want to think about which is more important – knowing a lot of the theory or practising just some of it.

BUDDHISM TODAY

Samye Ling Buddhist Temple, Eskdalemuir

Also in Scotland (and elsewhere) you'll find Buddhism sometimes becomes mixed up in people's minds with other things. Shops which sell Buddhist objects often sell 'new age'-type items as well. You might find a Buddha image right next to a set of Tarot cards, for example. People may do meditation which is based on Buddhist meditation but that won't make them Buddhists. Those who have chosen the faith as a way of life have varying views on this kind of adaptation of their faith.

So, to return to the earlier question: is Buddhism a religion or not? Something is usually considered to be a religion when it has:

◆ A set of beliefs involving a central core which all followers have some agreement with; in Buddhism this would be the basic teachings of Buddha, for example, the Four Noble Truths.

◆ A set of practices which, although they might vary within the faith, come to more or less the same thing; some kind of meditation is common to almost all forms of Buddhism.

◆ A set of moral values which may differ in detail but are common in spirit; in Buddhism this might be the idea of showing compassion to all living things.

◆ A shared history or set of traditions; all Buddhist groups originated with the teachings of Buddha Shakyamuni, the historical Buddha who was the man known previously as Siddartha Gautama. All modern forms of Buddhism rely essentially on his teachings.

Buddhism's spread was as much geographical as it was historical. Beginning in India, it spread around the world; as it spread it picked up elements of the cultures it mixed with. For example, in Tibet, Buddhism mixed with the local religion known as Bon, which was a shamanistic religion (with belief in spirits, ghosts, ceremonies for healing, supernatural elements). This blending led to 'gods' becoming part of Tibetan Buddhism.

Buddhism appears throughout the world in very different forms. Interestingly, quite a few film stars and people in the public eye seem to have become Buddhists recently. Because of its 'flexibility', Buddhism seems to be attracting people in the West who reject faiths which they seem to think don't have much room for personal choice.

But is it true that Buddhism lets you do your own thing? Is it really completely up to you what you take from it and what you don't? Are we living in a pick-and-mix world where people take the bits they like from a religion and not the bits they don't like? Is that acceptable? Does the rise of Buddhism in Scotland show that people are looking for some religious dimension to their lives? Do people really know what Buddhism is about, or are they attracted to it simply because it seems quite exotic?

Talk Point   A

Is there any evidence of the growth of Buddhism in your part of Scotland? Why do you think people are attracted to Buddhism?

A Brief History of Buddhism

Like all religions, Buddhism has a long and complex history. Its historical development is a mixture of the changes it experienced when it arrived in new places and the result of disagreements between its followers about what it should mean. As people understood the teaching of the Buddha in new ways, they set up their own forms of Buddhist practice which led to the development of different schools and sects of the faith and the wide variety of types of Buddhism around today. So here's the basic outline of how Buddhism grew and developed, and came to Scotland.

c. 480ʙᴄᴇ —— Death of the Buddha

Buddha's followers (Sangha) have been taught the Vinaya (rules and precepts) by the Buddha. These were not written down, so the first Buddhist Council takes place where one of the followers, Upali, recites the Vinaya from memory and another follower, Ananda, recites the Dhamma from his memory. These become the first two written scriptures of Buddhism.

As time goes on, other teachings of Buddha are remembered and added to the growing list of scriptures. But this leads to disagreement about what the Buddha actually meant.

c. 443–379ʙᴄᴇ —— Second Buddhist Council. Two groups of the Sangha split over differences of opinion. Mahasanghika (great-assembly-ites) parts ways with the Sthaviravadins (traditionalists). The Mahasanghikas don't think that the scriptures as they now are should be the final authority in Buddhist belief (later they become the Mahayana school of Buddhism).

c. 247ʙᴄᴇ —— Third Buddhist Council. King Ashoka in India has become Buddhist and sends out missionaries to spread Buddhism. This Council results in further disagreement and the development of other sects such as Sarvastivadin and Vibhajjavadin.

c. 240ʙᴄᴇ —— Vibhajjavadin community in Sri Lanka becomes the Theravada school of Buddhism.

Buddhism spreads further geographically. In China, it mixes with the religion of Taoism; in Tibet, it mixes with Shamanistic religions. It spreads further into South-East Asia and across to Japan.

480 ᴄᴇ —— The Buddhist missionary Bodhidharma travels to China, setting up Ch'an and Zen forms of Buddhism.

c. 650ᴄᴇ —— The first Buddhist temple is built in Tibet.

In countries where Buddhism is established, the faith's strength waxes and wanes throughout the years.

As Westerners travel the world (for example, discoverers like Marco Polo), Buddhist ideas encountered and taken home upon their return.

1893ᴄᴇ —— The World Parliament of Religions in Chicago is possibly the first notable encounter between Buddhism and the West.

Theosophical Society in UK and USA introduces some Buddhist ideas, though mixed with many other approaches to spirituality.

The First and Second World Wars lead to many UK soldiers coming into contact with Buddhist ideas as they are stationed in Buddhist countries.

Buddhist groups begin in UK, like the Tibetan Samye Ling in Eskdalemuir.

In 1967 an English monk, Sangharakshita, sets up the Friends of the Western Buddhist Order (FWBO). He feels that Buddhism does not need to be tied to any particular culture and should be less formal. He was stationed in India and Sri Lanka during the Second World War and was later ordained a Buddhist monk. The FWBO approaches Buddhism from a Western perspective and does not tie itself to 'exotic' or 'Eastern' ways of living the faith. FWBO involves beliefs and practices which combine Theravada, Zen and Tibetan traditions, although set in a Western context.

Sangharakshita, the founder of FWBO – probably not your mental image of a Buddhist monk!

Talk Point

B

Buddhism, like all religions, has many groups and subgroups. Do you think this is positive or negative?

Buddhism in the 21st Century: World – UK – Scotland – Your School

It is hard to work out how many Buddhists there are in the world today and where they are found because a Buddhist can follow the teachings of the Buddha without formally becoming part of any Buddhist group or organisation.

The website ***Buddhanet.net*** suggests that the number of Buddhists worldwide is around 360 million which is around 6% of the world's population. As with all religions, it's difficult to be certain about this because of how you might decide that someone is a member of a religion or not. Obviously those who choose it are, but this figure will also include those who are born into Buddhist families. Being a religious person might mean that you practise the religion faithfully or it might simply mean that you live in a place where that's the main religion and so it's yours too – even if you don't actively practise it.

Buddhists are found all over the world, but there are some places where it is stronger than others, as shown in the map on page 6. Generally speaking, Buddhism began in India and followed the major trade routes. Buddhism is most obvious now in Tibet and in South-East Asia, but it is also strong in areas of India and some of the islands in the Indian Ocean. Buddhism is also present in China, where vast numbers of people who practise it often practise it alongside other faiths as well – so they're not solely Buddhists.

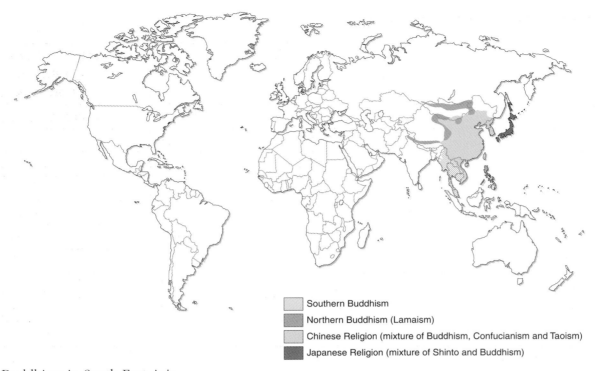

Southern Buddhism
Northern Buddhism (Lamaism)
Chinese Religion (mixture of Buddhism, Confucianism and Taoism)
Japanese Religion (mixture of Shinto and Buddhism)

Buddhism in South-East Asia

In contrast, the 2001 Census shows that about 0.3% of the total population in Great Britain is Buddhist.

Of the 149,000 Buddhists living in Britain in 2001, 36 per cent lived in London with the rest dispersed across the other regions. The highest concentrations of Buddhists were in the London boroughs of Westminster and Camden where they made up 1 per cent of the local population (Source: www.statistics.gov.uk).

In Scotland, there are many Buddhist organisations, found mostly in major towns and cities. The map opposite shows where FWBO Buddhist centres are.

Other forms of Buddhism are also found in Scotland, for example:

◆ The Heritage Buddhist Trust at Kelso in the Borders (members.aol.com/yeshiuk/index.html)

◆ A Soto Zen group in Portobello, Edinburgh (www.portobellobuddhist.org.uk)

◆ Rokpa Tibetan group in Dundee (www.dundee.rokpa.org)

◆ The Tharpaland Kadampa Retreat Centre in Dumfries (www.meditateinscotland.org)

In the Census of 2001, the Scottish Executive reports that 6800 people in Scotland are Buddhists. This number represents 0.13% of the whole Scottish population (which is less than the percentage throughout Great Britain). According to the 2001 Census, the religious make-up of those who are religious but do not follow Christianity in Scotland is as follows:

Population of Great Britain, by religion, April 2001

	Total population		Non-Christian religious population
	(Numbers)	(Percentages)	(Percentages)
Christian	41,014,811	71.8	
Muslim	1,588,890	2.8	51.9
Hindu	558,342	1.0	18.3
Sikh	336,179	0.6	11.0
Jewish	267,373	0.5	8.7
Buddhist	149,157	0.3	4.9
Any other religion	159,167	0.3	5.2
All non-Christian religious population	3,059,108	5.4	100.0
No religion	8,596,488	15.1	
Religion not stated	4,433,520	7.8	
All population	57,103,927	100.0	

Source: www.scotland.gov.uk/stats/bulletins/00398-02.asp

So, 7% of the religious non-Christian population of Scotland claim to be Buddhist (about 0.13% of the total population). Most of these people were brought up according to other faiths, so it's clear that many have deliberately chosen Buddhism as they have grown up rather than having been brought up in it.

Less than half of those people who currently practise Buddhism were brought up as Buddhists (46.1%). Other religious backgrounds of those currently practising Buddhism include Church of Scotland (16.3%), Other Christian religions (10.7%) and Roman Catholic (7.9%). A further 14.2% responded that they had no

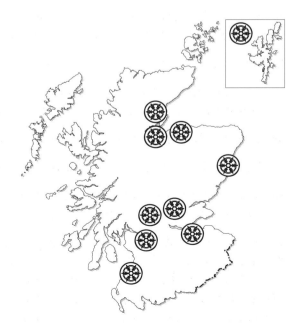

BUDDHISM TODAY

religious background (Source: www.scotland.gov.uk/stats/bulletins/00398-02.asp).

Interestingly, the Census also reports that 21% of people who now claim to have no religion at all were brought up as Buddhists. This is the highest figure in the country after Christianity (47%).

The following chart compares the age groups of people practising Buddhism with the age groups of other faiths in Scotland. The chart suggests that the most likely age group to be Buddhists in Scotland is the 30–49 age group.

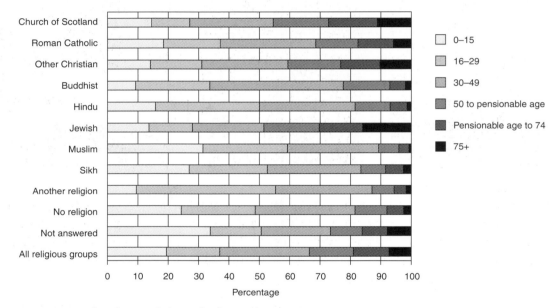

Source: www.scotland.gov.uk/stats/bulletins/00398-02.asp

Of course, one of the things about Buddhism – as you'll soon learn – is that people can be attracted to the lifestyle and teachings of Buddhism without necessarily becoming Buddhists!

Talk Point

Carry out a survey in your school to find out which religions are followed there. Be sensitive to people's feelings and make sure that it is anonymous. You could ask not only about who is a 'card carrying' Buddhist but also about people who are just attracted by Buddhist ideas. Survey pupils in a couple of schools – is yours more or less interested in Buddhism than others?

C

When we are born our parents have great hopes for us. Some of us turn out to be kind, helpful, generous people who make the world a better place. Others turn out to be nasty, selfish and even brutal. How does this happen? How does an innocent little baby turn out to be a mass murderer or a terrorist or someone who devotes their life the wellbeing of others?

There are many different views on human nature in psychology and philosophy. Different world religions also have different views on human nature. Humans like to know what makes us tick. Why do we do what we do? Why do we sometimes do things even though we know we shouldn't? How do we tell right from wrong? What should we believe about life? Where do our beliefs come from? Why do we even think up questions like this?

One of the reasons you are doing RMPS is because you are interested in these kinds of questions. What are people all about? What are we aiming for in life? How do we get what we can out of our short time here on Earth? (Do you exist in some form after death?) This course covers all of these big questions. You'll know them as:

◆ The Human Condition

◆ The Goals

◆ The Means.

Now why would you want to find out what Buddhism teaches about these three issues? Buddhism might seem quite remote to you – a faith from far away lands – or you might think it's just something which people who used to be 'hippies' are into.

Buddhism, like all religions of the world, has a long history of thinking through these kinds of questions and suggesting answers. It can't force you to accept these answers (as you will see, Buddhism is not the kind of religion that forces anybody to do anything), but it can get you thinking about your own response to these answers. That's what this book is about. There's not much point in just learning a series of facts about Buddhist belief – it has to make you think about your own views. Buddhism suggests answers to all these three issues, and it's up to you whether you take them or leave them. But you can't do anything if you don't know what the (questions and) answers are in the first place.

When you look around the world today, for example, watch TV, read the papers or browse the Internet, you might be forgiven for thinking that the world is pretty messed up and that most of our problems are caused by the actions of humans.

Think back to the last time you did something wrong (for most of us it probably wasn't that long ago) and ask yourself: Why did I do that? You probably knew it was wrong even as you were doing it. Now ask yourself: What made it wrong – was it the intention of what you did or the consequence? And how did it affect you as well as the person or thing you did it to?

What is being a human actually about? Is there such a thing as the human condition? Have Buddhists got the explanation for this right? Is what you'll find in this book the key to one of the most important things there is – understanding yourself?

Why does one baby turn out to be a hero and the other a killer? What's the difference between humans and everything else? What is the unique job of humans? What, in fact, is the meaning of life? The Buddhist faith suggests answers to these questions. Read on.

Getting into it

Think through the following questions. It's up to you and your teacher whether you write answers to them, discuss them, turn them into role play, dramas, essays, pieces of artwork, etc.

◆ What is special about being human?

◆ Is there such a thing as human nature?

◆ Are you actually real in the first place?

◆ Is everything an illusion?

◆ Is life full of suffering?

◆ What causes suffering and how can it be ended?

◆ Why do humans do good or bad things?

◆ What counts as good or bad?

◆ Are we living in ignorance?

◆ Is this our only life or are there more to come (and were there more before this one)?

◆ How do our beliefs affect our actions?

◆ Is there a God?

◆ Are there gods?

◆ Do we have a soul?

◆ Should we spend any time thinking about human nature or is it a waste of time?

◆ What is the point of life? (Is there one?)

Buddhist Belief and Action

BUDDHAWORLD!

Coming soon! An experience all five of your skhandas won't forget.
BUDDHAWORLD!!!

YES! An adventure for the entire enlightened family! Book now for our non-stop flights from Inverness or Stornoway to exotic KATHMANDU, the mystical city of faith, mountains and BUDDHAWORLD!

IMAX theatres (with 70 ft screens) bring you the story of Siddartha Gautama, rebel with the cause of freeing all beings from suffering! THRILL to the sheltered young Siddartha's escape from the watch of his father's guards. GASP as he witnesses death, decay and suffering (with Dolby sound and mind-blowing special effects). BUY the Siddartha T-shirt, lunchbox and soundtrack.

WONDER at the actual site where the young Buddha was born for the last time, purchase lotus flowers and the 'Buddha is Born' DVD. (Buddha's rebirths I, II, III, IV, V, VI and all other versions available too.)

STAY in authentically sparsely furnished rooms, each featuring no beds, begging bowls and complimentary orange robes for that special Buddhist occasion.

PAT the belly of the 250 foot simulated-gold-covered smiling Buddha while a photographer records the moment (additional cost). EXPERIENCE the thrilling ride through the realms on Kamma Mountain – the World's Fastest, Tallest ride through the many realms of existence. BE TERRIFIED BY the spooky Hell Realm! COWER at the Hungry Ghosts Realm! BE DAZZLED BY the God Realm (premium rate rides only)! EXPERIENCE your very own virtual rebirth and come home with your own unique Kamma certificate.

Reserve now!

Full refunds available – if you don't like the Dhamma, try something else instead!

Source: based on an idea by Dan Diaz at
www.serve.com/cmtan/buddhism/Lighter/buddhaworld.html

Don't just do something, sit there

Like many religions, Buddhism suffers from being misunderstood. Many non-Buddhists think of it as a religion where people do little but sit around meditating all the time. Others think it is only about 'finding yourself' or seeking your own answers to life. Some aspects of Buddhism are very confusing to a 'Western' way of thinking. For example, Zen koans seem meaningless to some people and the practice of monks living off the donations of others doesn't fit very well with our get-up-and-do-it society. To many people, the basic principles of Buddhism, for example, trying to become less attached to life, the universe and everything, seem like the opposite of life, which they might think is all about getting and keeping things and doing well for yourself. Do Buddhists have aims? Are they selfish? Do they 'do' anything useful? Do they need to? All of these questions are difficult to answer, because they all rely on the idea that ultimately there is a point to life. But is there? Can we know it? Does it make a difference to how we live it?

Talk Point   1

What views are there already about Buddhists and Buddhism in your class?

Zen Buddhist View

A Zen master once said to me, 'Do the opposite of whatever I tell you.' So I didn't.

Source: www.serve.com/cmtan/buddhism/Lighter/comments.html

THE HUMAN CONDITION

A Cup of Tea

Nan-in, a Japanese master during the Meiji era (1868–1912), received a university professor who came to inquire about Zen.

Nan-in served tea. He poured his visitor's cup full, and then kept on pouring.

The professor watched the overflow until he no longer could restrain himself. 'It is overfull. No more will go in!'

'Like this cup,' Nan-in said, 'you are full of your own opinions and speculations. How can I show you Zen unless you first empty your cup?'

Buddhists definitely meditate – but is that all they do? Many Buddhists believe that your life must be *lived* rather than just *understood*. Once you have begun to follow the middle path of the Buddha's teachings then this right way of *thinking* will lead to a right way of *being*. This is cause and effect. Buddhists, like many religious groups, have those who are very much engaged in the big issues of life. Buddhists help others, carry out acts of charity, work, and live alongside you and me. Their way of life isn't about staring inwards all the time, but they do think it is important to reflect on life and try to understand it so that it means something more than just thoughtlessly treading the same old paths every day.

If it works for you...

'If you don't like it, you know what you can do with it.' These weren't the actual words of the Buddha, but they are, more or less, what he meant. The Buddha made it clear to his followers that they were not to accept what he said just because he had said it. They were to try things out for themselves. After the Buddha became a holy man following his experience of the four sights, he tried various faiths and practices of his time. He found all of them to be unsatisfactory, until he found his own 'middle way' between a variety of extremes. This approach became quite central to the Buddhist lifestyle. If you try something out and it doesn't seem to be for you, then you should give it up and try something else out instead. Now Buddhism has teachers and scriptures of varying levels of importance and holiness. It has traditions, ethical values and history – all the things which most religions share. However, the bottom line of Buddhism is 'suck it and see'. Buddhists believe that the Buddha lets each individual choose their own way to understand the Dhamma. There aren't any absolute rules about that, even although there are many rules, laws and precepts which different kinds of Buddhists will make themselves follow. Buddhism isn't really all about 'metaphysical' questions like what happens after death and what is the meaning of life. It is about living out your life in action – putting the Dhamma into practice in your daily life so that your life improves.

In fact, the Buddha simply refused to answer certain questions because he thought that they were pointless and that thinking about them was likely to get in the way of the person living out the Dhamma. The 'point' of life is to get rid of craving and so to escape the endless cycle of rebirth. The Buddha's own teaching arose from his experience of the world, not from reading holy books or listening to teachers. He suggested that we're all likely to learn best this way. The Buddha claimed that if you spent your entire life thinking about philosophical questions, then you'd never have any time to do the practical things that will help you renounce craving and stop the cycle of rebirth.

Time Out　　　　　　　　　　　　　　　　　　　1

In your opinion, is learning by experience the best way to learn? What possible problems might there be with it?

God: big G or little g?

Whether to write God or god is a really difficult question in relation to Buddhism. Generally speaking, in the West when people write the word God, they mean some kind of monotheistic deity; this means a being, of which there is only one, and which is both the cause of everything and is in charge of everything. This roughly matches up with the God of Islam, Christianity and Judaism as well as Hinduism. Each of these faiths gives their God a different name, but whatever the name, the meaning is the same: their God is the one and only supreme being. Now Christianity gets a bit complicated because it has Jesus and the Holy Spirit with God, forming the Holy Trinity. Is this three Gods or one? Answering that question is not a relevant task for this book (but you may find it helpful to look at the Christianity book in this series). Hinduism talks about different aspects of God, like Krishna and Shiva, and tends to call these gods (that is, with a small g).

What does Buddhism do? At first sight everything seems clear and simple. Buddhists don't believe in God-with-a-big-G. There is no supreme being controlling all and from which everything began. Everything is cause and effect. One thing causes another. There is no being above it all or in a heaven pulling the strings and making decisions about right and wrong, heaven and hell and that kind of thing. In Buddhism, every human being makes their own lives good or bad. Nothing is decided for us or has been decided beforehand. Everything we experience is as a result of human actions. This is one reason why Buddhism is very popular in the West, where individual freedom is very highly valued.

THE HUMAN CONDITION

Talk Point

2

From what you know of other world faiths, is it fair to say that their belief in a God results in humans being less free to choose to act as they want?

The Buddhist view of the Buddha

Buddhists believe [Buddha] reached a state of being that goes beyond anything else in the world. If normal experience is based on conditions — upbringing, psychology, opinions, perceptions — Enlightenment is Unconditioned. A Buddha is free from greed, hatred and ignorance, and characterised by wisdom, compassion and freedom. Enlightenment brings insight into the deepest workings of life, and therefore into the cause of human suffering; the problem that had initially set him on his spiritual quest. [...] The Buddha was not a god and he made no claim to divinity. He was a human being who, through tremendous effort of heart and mind, transformed all limitations. He affirmed the potential of every being to reach Buddhahood. Buddhists see him as an ideal human being, and a guide who can lead us all towards Enlightenment.

Source: www.fwbo.org/buddha.html

The importance of local belief systems

Some people in the West who are attracted to Buddhism find some versions of Buddhism more difficult to understand than others. Although the Buddha wasn't a God (or even a god), and he never suggested that he was, modern Buddhism is a strange mixture of the Dhamma which the Buddha taught and rituals,

customs and traditions of religions which already existed in places where Buddhism eventually took root. Tibetan Buddhists, for example, mix the teachings of the Buddha with worship of mountains and superstitious rituals to bring good fortune. In some parts of Asia, Buddhists mix the teachings of the Buddha with good luck charms and practices from completely different religions. In many forms of Buddhism there are demi-gods and goddesses – supernatural beings, good and bad spirits, helpful and spiteful ghosts, and so on. Some Buddhists, like those from the Zen tradition, are very stark and austere, whereas other forms of Buddhism are very ornate, colourful and lively.

We probably shouldn't be too surprised by this variety. This is the way most religions spread. They don't just push out what came before; instead they gradually replace it, often still holding on to some of the ideas of the 'old ways'. Some Buddhists believe that praying to or worshipping such gods-with-a-little-g can help you along the path to Enlightenment and so help you escape rebirth. Some believe that the Buddha and other Buddha-like beings can help you along too. Still others believe that these are colourful and sometimes helpful ways to help you focus on meditation, but that your Enlightenment can only come through your own actions. This is, therefore, the major difference between Buddhism and other faiths (although as you've seen, it's not that simple because some Buddhists do think that gods can help you): for most Buddhists, your life is what *you* make it. You can't turn to a god for help, nor has this god dealt you a set of cards which will decide how well you do in the game of life. It's up to you.

Talk Point 3

Do you think it's helpful for religions to adopt parts of the culture of countries they move into? Can you think of any examples in the UK? (Clue: think about the worship of saints in the Christian church.)

Was the Buddha a god?

No, he was not. He did not claim that he was a god, the child of a god or even the messenger from a god. He was a man who perfected himself and taught that if we follow his example, we could perfect ourselves also.

Source: Ven. S. Dhammika at www.buddhanet.net/ans5.htm

Don't just sit there, do something: the Dhamma

Buddhists tend to be quite practical. Although the theory of Buddhism and its philosophy can be very complex and hard to grasp, Buddhists don't see it as a completely intellectual activity. Although you definitely need your brain to understand the theories of Buddhism, if you sit around just thinking about it all day you probably won't get very far in developing a Buddhist life. Buddhists think that beliefs lead to actions. What you *do* is equally important as what you *think*. Non-Buddhists have the mistaken notion that Buddhism involves just sitting around all day thinking about quite selfish things. But Buddhists would not agree, believing that what you think matters, but so does what you do after all that thinking.

Living a Buddhist life is quite simple and follows fairly straightforward principles. By definition it can't be selfish. If you only ever thought about yourself then you'd be a poor Buddhist. For example, one of the key elements of Buddhism is concern for the happiness and wellbeing of other living creatures. You won't be paying much attention to the wellbeing of others if you're totally self-obsessed. The Dhamma, or the teaching of the Buddha, is all about helping others along the way (and by doing so helping yourself too). Buddhism requires you to be selfless, and that, some Buddhists would argue, is the whole point.

Me, I, myself, and other illusions

You can only be selfish or selfless if there's a self in the first place. (More of that later.) Buddhists believe that what makes you *you* is not as obvious as you might think, and this leads to the concept of Anatta (no soul). What is you is difficult to pin down because it is changing minute by minute. Just think, in the time it has taken you to read to the end of this sentence your thoughts have changed and cells in your body may have died and new ones grown. Your digestive system is also turning the last thing you ate into you. So, in some ways, *you* are an illusion. But even if you are, you're an illusion with the potential to think and do the right things or the wrong things. How does a Buddhist know which is which and what is what? It's simple: the Buddha has already told us.

Activities

Knowledge, Understanding, Evaluation

1 Explain the instruction by the Zen master.

2 How could someone use Nan-in's teachings to support the teaching of RMPS?

3 Do you think it is important to reflect upon life rather than just living it? Explain your answer.

4 What did the Buddha teach about what you should do with his teaching?

5 Why do Buddhists put the Dhamma into action?

6 From what you have read so far, should Buddhists study Buddhism?

7 Does Buddhism have a God?

8 Does Buddhism have gods?

9 What Buddhist belief suggests that human free choice is important?

10 According to the FWBO quote, was the Buddha a god?

11 Why might some people be attracted to a godless religion?

12 What evidence is there in this section that modern Buddhism includes many different ideas and practices?

13 Do you think it's good for religions to adopt things from other religions and beliefs? Explain your answer.

14 From what you have read so far, do you think Buddhism is a selfish or selfless religion?

15 From what you have read so far, do you think Buddhism is a religion?

Practical Activities

1 Use a world map to display the varieties of Buddhism in the world today. Include information about the different kinds of Buddhism you're likely to find in different countries.

2 Find out about two Buddhist places of worship, preferably one from the Zen tradition and one from the Tibetan tradition. Describe each and make clear the similarities and differences. You could do this as a display if you like.

3 Design your own poster for 'Buddha World!'

4 Get some photos of yourself through time and display them. For each one describe your personality at the time, and the kinds of things you thought and did. Is there any consistent thread running through them all? Do you think you were the same 'self' all that time?

5 Design a leaflet encouraging Scottish people to become Buddhists. What might be attractive about Buddhism for them?

Unit Assessment Question

Int 1 Is it true to say that Buddhists do not believe in God? *(4)*

Int 2 Should a Buddhist follow the teachings of Buddha just because he taught them? *(4)*

Higher

'For Buddhists, freedom of choice in what you believe is central.' Would a Buddhist agree? *(6)*

THE HUMAN CONDITION

Sample Exam Question

Int 1 'Buddhists believe that beliefs should lead to actions.' How might a Buddhist explain this statement? *(4AE)*

Int 2 'Everything we experience is the result of human actions.' Would a Buddhist agree? *(6AE)*

Higher

What might a Buddhist say was the value of following the teachings of the Buddha? *(4AE)*

Homework

Find out about at least one famous Buddhist from popular entertainment (film, TV, music, sport, etc.). Explain how compatible you think their lifestyle is with Buddhism from what you know about the religion so far.

Personal Reflection

How attractive is Buddhism to you? Can you see yourself as a Buddhist? (If you are already a Buddhist, what is it about Buddhism which keeps you a Buddhist?)

Buddha's Early Life: The Four Noble Truths

The story of Kisagotami

Kisagotami was, to put it mildly, a bit of a babe. But she wasn't up to hard work and so was treated quite badly by her family, a bit like Cinderella. But because she was so pure dead gorgeous, she nabbed a man and she went to live with him and his family. Sadly, her husband's family also treated her badly and her life was miserable, until she gave birth to a son. After this, everyone respected her and her life improved and she was much happier.

Her son grew to be strong and handsome. But one day he was playing in the forest when a snake bit him and he died. Kisagotami was wild with grief. She wouldn't sleep, wouldn't eat and just went crazy. She wandered round the village with her dead son's body, screaming for medicine to make him better. Folks shook their heads, saying 'She's lost the plot.' But one old man took pity on her. He was a follower of Siddartha Gautama, the Buddha. He said to her, 'The Buddha is in the next village. Maybe he could give you medicine for your dead son. You never know, it's worth a try, eh?'

So off she went through the cold night, carrying her son. Next day she found the Buddha among a crowd. People moved out of her way, not wanting to be too close to a nutter with a dead boy in her arms.

'They say you're something special, Mr Buddha. Can you give me medicine to bring my son back to me?'

Buddha looked at her with kindness. 'Go to the city. Bring me one grain of mustard seed from every house that death has not visited. I'll be here when you get back.'

So off she went. But at every house she heard story after story of death, suffering and misery. She heard of the deaths of the old, the young, the beautiful and the plain. Of wives and husbands, brothers, sisters best friends. All who were left behind felt just the same as her.

And so she understood.

She returned to the Buddha. Neither of them said a word. She had already taken the boy's body to the place where they cremated the dead.

Talk Point

4

What did Kisagotami learn and why did she come to accept the death of her child? Would you have reacted the same way?

Learning and teaching compassion

The Buddha taught Kisagotami to accept what had happened to her son. Whereas many people might have just told her to get over it, and some might have tried to give a lengthy explanation about how death is inevitable, the Buddha helped her find it all out for herself. He didn't give her a big philosophical lecture, he just told her to go and learn by experience. This is a very common approach in Buddhism and in the teachings of the Buddha himself. He probably knew that a grieving mother was in no fit state to think logically about what had happened to her son, but she could learn through listening to others and coming to understand more with her heart than her head. Kisagotami learned through her own experience that sometimes there aren't any obvious answers to life's big questions other than that's just the way it is, and that acceptance of this is the way forward.

When you really think about it, this is first class teaching. The Buddha knew that Kisagotami would have to come to terms with things in her own way. Death has always been around and always will be – it'll get us all in the end – but that's just the way things are. He knew that she would have to understand this for herself; someone telling her would just have been empty words as far as she was concerned. So he sent her off so she would find her own little bit of understanding, in this case that there are certain things in life that you just have to accept.

Time Out

2

In groups, discuss a time when you, or someone you know, learned to accept something that you had found difficult to accept. How did you learn to accept the way things sometimes are?

The life of Siddartha Gautama

The story of the Buddha's life, like that of all great religious figures, is a complicated mixture of ordinary everyday things and extraordinary supernatural events. It is said that there was once a king called Suddhodana and a queen named Mahamaya who lived in the city of Kapilavastu in the sixth century BCE. One day, the Queen dreamt that a white elephant carrying a lotus entered her side. Soon after this her son Siddartha was born. Some astrologers predicted that

he would either become a great ruler or a holy man. The King, his father, wanted Siddartha to follow in his footsteps and be a ruler, not a holy man, so he took some fairly drastic action. He decided that the only reason his son would go off and become a holy man was if he found out that life for most people was very hard, so he kept his son in splendid isolation throughout his young life. Siddartha had everything he wanted without question; and any kind of decay, illness and sadness were removed before he ever saw them. He had a truly charmed life.

Talk Point

5

Imagine you live in a palace and have absolutely every desire fulfilled, except for one thing: you are not allowed to go outside the palace. How important would it be for you to get out? Or would you just stay there and soak up all the pleasure?

After a time, Siddartha married a beautiful princess and they had a son, Rahula. Everything was just perfect for him. However, according to Buddhist tradition, Siddartha decided that he wanted to see how other people outside the palace lived and he persuaded his servant to take him secretly into the village. There are different versions of this story but each one contains the 'four sights'. These sights made Siddartha realise what real life was like for most other people, in stark contrast to his life of privilege. In the village he saw four things. The first thing he saw was old age. He'd never seen someone so old that they were decrepit. He came to understand that most of us get that way. He also saw sickness – real harrowing disease and illness, and he wondered why this happened. Then he saw death. His servant explained to him that old age, sickness and death happen to everyone and are just part of existence. Siddartha was shocked by all of these revelations. Finally, he saw a holy man and learned that such people spend their time trying to help people make sense of old age, sickness and death. Then and there he decided that he wanted to become a holy man too. The astrologers had been right after all.

Talk Point　　　　　　　　　　　　　　　　　　　　6

Does a story have to be true before you can learn from it?

What's it all about?

Siddartha Gautama was a real person. But does this story accurately describe what actually happened? Some Buddhists think that the events of this story happened just as they are written. So the story has a *literal* meaning. Siddartha did live a sheltered life and did go down to the village secretly. On each occasion he saw something else which helped him build up a better picture of the sorry world in which he lived. Sometimes truth is stranger than fiction and a boy who had been so sheltered and spoiled would have been completely shocked by seeing the reality of life like that. It would have shaken his whole way of looking at life. Sometimes we just have to see things we do not expect for us to change what we do or think.

Another explanation for the story is that Siddartha slowly came to realise that life is full of these things even though he had been sheltered from them all his life until that point. In this interpretation, the story just helps to give a good mental picture of the things Siddartha found to be wrong with the world, so the story has *symbolic* meaning. As Siddartha matured he realised that things weren't as he thought they were. Perhaps he simply reached a point in his life where the search for the meaning of it all was far more important than the life of pleasure he led. It's not unusual for people to spend all their life trying to achieve their idea of wealth and success only to realise that it's not always all that satisfying once they actually have it.

What Siddartha did next

Siddartha saw a holy man too on his visits to the village. He believed this holy man had a better understanding of the three evils he'd witnessed than he had. So, he decided to become a holy man too. But which kind? In Siddartha's world, holy men were common and came in all shapes, sizes and forms of belief. Siddartha, after all, lived in a Hindu world where superstitions, philosophy, theologies, charms and rituals all existed side by side in a rather odd mixture.

To become a holy man, however, first he had to leave home. There is a story that he left after a great party, where he woke up after a short sleep to find all the people in the room asleep, snoring and ugly. These people had been beautiful in his mind at the start of the party and now he saw them differently and this made his mind up to go. He found his wife asleep with their baby son in her arms. He took one last look – and left. To be a holy man meant that you had to give up all your attachments to the life you had lived before, even your family.

As was the practice he found himself a teacher – or guru – who would guide him to find answers to the questions of why we grow old, sick and eventually die. First he tried Alara Kalama, then Uddaka and finally he joined up with five friends, Kondanna, Bhaddiya, Vappa, Mahanama and Assaji, and spent six years living as an ascetic. This meant that he tried to find the answers through self-punishment, by starving and hurting himself; it is said that he even tried holding his breath until his ears stung with pain. In all of this he found no answers and gave up this approach.

Eventually, he decided that he would sit and think until the answers to his questions came, and that's exactly what he did. He found a tree and sat under it and meditated. During this time, the evil one, Mara, tried to tempt him away from his meditations – but he stayed still.

THE HUMAN CONDITION

Temptations of Mara 1

The night before the Buddha attained final enlightenment, Mara was there to tempt him. Buddha was tempted by Mara. Mara is the tempter. He always wanted the Buddha to be a politician, to be a king, or a president, or a foreign minister, or running a business, having a lot of money, a lot of beautiful women; and he was always trying to tempt the Buddha so that Buddha would go into these directions. That is Mara.

Source: Thich Nhat Hanh at www.buddhistinformation.com/mara_and_the_buddha.htm

Temptations of Mara 2

Centuries ago the coming Buddha sat under the Bodhi-tree and vowed not to move until he learned to eradicate suffering, unfolding Anuttara Samyak Sambodhi, the Consummation of Incomparable Enlightenment. But Mara, the personification of evil, tried to usurp his plans by sending his three daughters Tanha (desire), Raga (lust), and Arati (aversion), to seduce him and break his concentration. However, the coming Buddha was too strong for Mara.

Source: www.angelfire.com/electronic/bodhidharma/mara.html

Some Buddhists think of the temptations of Mara as a literal event, where a real Mara actually tried to persuade Siddartha away from the good path he was about to follow. They see Mara as a prince of darkness-like figure. In Theravadin countries, it is important to please the spirits, so perhaps Mara was (and still is) a real being intent on stirring up nasty stuff. Others think of the temptations of Mara as a symbolic event, showing the coming Buddha fighting with his own human nature, a human nature which is inclined to fool itself and hide from Reality. In this symbolic interpretation, Mara represents the personification of evil within us and around us.

Whether or not the story is literally true, the meaning is clear. Old age, sickness and death are three things which wealth and power cannot fight. Not only that, but wealth and power don't help you in the least to understand what these are all about. Siddartha decided that the answer to these three fundamental problems in life must lie somewhere else. He fought off the temptations of being human to seek a better way. According to Buddhists he found it and decided to pass it on to everyone.

Talk Point

7

Have you ever had an experience where something which had been confusing before just fell into place and became clear?

Time Out (3)

Discuss in class: does Mara exist?

Eventually, Siddartha understood. Imagine a bucket full of water and mud all stirred up; eventually the mud settles to the bottom and the water becomes clear. That's probably how it was for Siddartha – everything simply became clear. Siddartha had found the answer to the problems of old age, sickness and death. He had lit up in his own mind what before had been in darkness – he was Enlightened. From now on he would be the Buddha – the Enlightened One.

At dawn on the day of his Enlightenment he uttered these words:

Thro' many a birth in samsara wandered
Seeking, but not finding, the builder of this house.
Sorrowful is repeated birth.
House builder, thou art seen.
Thou shalt build no house again.
All thy rafters are broken; thy ridgepole is shattered.
The mind attains the unconditioned.
Achieved is the end of craving.

The Dhammapada 153–154

What he discovered in that moment of Enlightenment is the subject of the rest of this book...

The Four Noble Truths

Rab has gone to visit his friend Donnie. The last time they saw each other they had just been kicked out of a nightclub in Inverness where they had tried something rather bizarre with a cream egg. Donnie has had a bit of a change of lifestyle, and as Rab's car turns the last country corner, the scene changes from the Dumfries countryside to a beautiful Tibetan temple. Donnie is at Samye Ling, trying to find himself. Rab thinks that should be easy given the amount of time he's spending looking at his own belly button. After the customary greetings, they sit down to a cup of tea and a carob bar.

RAB: Well, Donnie, quite sumthin this place eh?
DONNIE: Aye, very harmonic Rab.
RAB: Aye, harmonic right enough. Ah like yer baldy by the way, but are ye no freezing in that purple blanket?
DONNIE: Ah'm tryin to detach myself from worldly things.
RAB: You huvny got any worldly things – the bailiffs took them aff ye tae pay all yer credit cards.

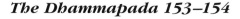

27

DONNIE: Indeed Rab – so I'm now free of the burden of wealth.

RAB: I don't remember it exactly weighin you doon. So Buddhism is it – loads of chanting and dancing round bonfires in yer herbal wellies...?

DONNIE: Not exactly Rab. It's more about how ye see things. Wakin up and opening yer eyes tae what's around you.

RAB: Looks a lot like trees, fields, and folks in scratchy jumpers tae me.... country folks full of eastern promise.

DONNIE: No, the inner things Rab. Lightin up our darkness. Seeking Nirvana.

RAB: You had their albums – they went with the bailiffs – they were vinyl too – probably worth a bit nowadays.

DONNIE: No, Rab – the meaning of life. Understanding whit it's all aboot.

RAB: And you're goin tae get that here?

DONNIE: I could get it anywhere – but here's a good place for the moment.

RAB: So, huv they told ye yet what the meaning of life is, or do you have tae become a black belt in Buddhism or sumthin first?

DONNIE: The meaning of life comes down tae the four Noble Truths.

RAB: Which are?

DONNIE: First: Life is full of suffering. Everywhere ye look there's misery. Even when ye think things are great you're foolin yerself. At the end of the day, it's all just glum.

RAB: Ah thought this place was supposed to make ye happy?

DONNIE: Happiness is no more real than sadness.

RAB: You've lost me now. So, what causes all this doom and gloom, Noble Truth number 2 I suppose?

DONNIE: Dead right Rab. Suffering is caused by the fact that we're always wantin things and these things canny be satisfied. Life isny going to be the way we want it to be and as long as we want it that way we'll suffer.

RAB: So we just stop wantin...?

DONNIE: Very difficult. It's human nature tae want – tae crave – like when you gave up smokin' – remember those cravings? Well that's what we're like aboot everythin in life.

RAB: So there's nae answer... It's all hopeless... you're here tae hide from it all...? Life's just gloom and that's that?

DONNIE: No Rab, there's nae hidin from it all. But ye can stop the craving – it just depends how ye look at it.

RAB: Is that baldy you've got freezing yer brain and makin it slow down here, Donnie? Suffering and misery will still happen no matter how ye 'look at it'.

DONNIE: True, they will, but that's no the point. That gets me tae the third Noble Truth. Ye huv tae realise that nothin lasts. The good stuff, like yer team winning the Scottish Cup, or the bad stuff like whit that lassie in Inverness told ye to dae with yer cream egg. They all pass. Nothin stays the same. Once ye get a handle on that, you'll realise that the craving dies doon. If you hang on tae things, they'll hang on tae you, weighing ye doon. That keeps suffering going. Letting go of it is the way tae handle it. Then ye huv got Nirvana.

RAB: So, is there a secret code aboot this somewhere, like that Da Vinci thing – is it stuck on the back of a painting in the Kelvingrove?

DONNIE: No, it's much more simple. The fourth Noble Truth gives ye a way tae stop craving, but it's no easy. It's the Noble Eightfold Path. Eight simple steps to kick the habit of craving.

RAB: Is that like the three steps tae heaven that Showaddywaddy did?

Donnie just gives Rab a withering stare

DONNIE: No, it's just eight rules for livin which help tae stop the craving.

RAB: Hey, that's a bit like they patches I used when ah was giving up the fags.

DONNIE: If I remember right, you used a lot more than eight of them . . . and all at the same time . . . but yes, Rab, I suppose that's exactly what it's like. . .

RAB: By the way, are ye allowed tae have a wee drag here. . .?

Four steps to Nibbana

After Siddartha's Enlightenment, he becomes the Buddha, the Enlightened One. His eyes are truly open to the way things are and what to do about them. Donnie is quite new to the Buddhist lifestyle and so he's not using the language quite correctly yet, but his understanding of the Four Noble Truths is pretty sound. The Four Noble Truths are:

◆ The First Noble Truth: Dukkha

◆ The Second Noble Truth: Samudaya

◆ The Third Noble Truth: Nirodha

◆ The Fourth Noble Truth: Magga

The First Noble Truth: Dukkha

The First Noble Truth is: life is full of suffering. You only have to pick up a newspaper to see the truth of this. Buddhists refer to this as Dukkha, but it is a little more complex than just suffering. It includes obvious examples of suffering,

such as illness, death and being dumped by text message, but it's more than that. It includes the whole idea that nothing ever really satisfies you. When you don't get what you want you suffer because it's out of reach. Your longing for it gets in the way of everything else. When you get what you want, does the suffering (wanting) stop? Maybe, temporarily. But eventually it comes back, because then you want something else or you realise that the thing you wanted (and got) wasn't what you thought it was going to be.

THE HUMAN CONDITION

The Buddha's first sermon: on suffering

What, O monks, is the Noble Truth of Suffering? Birth is suffering, sickness is suffering, old age is suffering, death is suffering. Pain, grief, sorrow, lamentation and despair are suffering. [...] The five factors of individuality are suffering.

Source: The Buddha's first sermon

Time Out

1 Think back to your childhood, to a toy you longed for and which looked so enticing on TV or even on the box of packaging. When you got it, were you just as pleased with the real thing? How long did you play with it?

2 Take a mental walk around your possessions at home. Which ones were things you couldn't wait to get? How many of them are still things you have any interest in? Has your craving really been satisfied? Did getting it stop you from wanting something else?

So, for Buddhists, suffering is built into the system. It's very difficult to avoid. Even the good things in life involve suffering, if only because we realise things can't always be like this. When did you last try to recreate the conditions where something good happened to you? Did you manage? The very fact that happiness doesn't last is in itself a form of suffering.

What 'suffering' means

Suffering is a . . . very misleading translation of the word *dukkha*, for the Buddha acknowledged that life was not just one long vale of tears, but it also had its moments of happiness. What he was saying was that when a human life is looked at overall, it is clear that what we might call a permanent state of *angst*, which stems from what we want and hope for ourselves, is *systematically* built into it.

Source: The Essence of Buddhism, by Jo Durden Smith

The Second Noble Truth: Samudaya

The Second Noble Truth is: suffering is caused by desire. Buddhists call this desire Tanha, which literally means thirst. When you want something it has a hold on you. Perhaps it blinds you to everything else. Perhaps what you do to try to achieve isn't helpful for you or others. Perhaps it's something which it would be very difficult for you to achieve and so in wanting it so desperately you're pointlessly beating yourself up about something you can do nothing about. The craving itself becomes a source of suffering. This desire is also pointless because ultimately it cannot be fulfilled. There is no logical end to desire because every time one desire is fulfilled another pops up right away to take its place. So although individual desires might be satisfied, desire itself never can be.

The Buddha's first sermon: on cause of suffering

This, O Monks, is the Truth of the Arising of Suffering. It is this thirst or craving (tanha) which gives rise to rebirth, which is bound up with passion and delight and which seeks fresh pleasure now here and now there in the form of thirst for sensual pleasure, thirst for existence and thirst for non-existence.

Source: The Buddha's first sermon

The Third Noble Truth (Nirodha)

The Third Noble Truth is: to stop suffering you have to stop desiring. Once this has happened you have achieved the state of Nibbana. The aim is not to satisfy your desire by achieving it, but never to have the desire in the first place. Nibbana is where you have reached a state of transcendence. In other words, you have turned the tables on the things you could desire. You have put yourself out of *their* reach by not wanting them. Once you're out of their reach, they no longer have a hold on you and so you no longer suffer. This sense of non-attachment is one of the key things Buddhists seek. For as long as you are attached to things you are caught up in the troubles of life. Once you detach yourself from them you aren't caught up any more.

THE HUMAN CONDITION

THE HUMAN CONDITION

The Buddha's first sermon: on stopping suffering

This, O Monks, is the Truth of the Cessation of Suffering. It is the utter cessation of that craving (tanha), the withdrawal from it, the renouncing of it, the rejection of it, liberation from it, non-attachment to it.

Source: The Buddha's first sermon

Talk Point

Have you ever had an experience where suddenly, something which you were very focused upon, just didn't seem to matter any more? Have you ever come to realise that something was far less important than you had thought it was? How did you feel at that point?

So how do you develop this detachment, and should you desire it? Buddhists believe that becoming detached from Tanha involves a set of practical steps focusing on different aspects of your life. It's not just about changing the way you *think* but about changing the way you *are*.

The Fourth Noble Truth (Magga)

The Fourth Noble Truth is the Noble Eightfold Path. It isn't a single statement like the other Noble Truths; it is a set of steps leading to a state of existence where you are detached from desire and so no longer crave and so no longer suffer. The steps don't come in any order and there's no test for whether you have achieved them or not because they last throughout your life. Suffering happens throughout life, in little ways, moment by moment. So, to free yourself from suffering you have to have the Eightfold Path constantly in your mind so that it's second nature – it's just the way you live.

The Noble Eightfold Path is about how you choose to live and respond to what life throws at you, covering all of life's activities. Buddhists believe that if you follow the Eightfold Path properly, then your life will be free of suffering and you will have attained Nibbana.

The Buddha's first sermon: the Eightfold Path

This, O Monks, is the Truth of the Path which leads to the cessation of suffering. It is the Noble Eightfold Path which consists of [...]

Source: The Buddha's first sermon

Reality and the Human Condition

Siddartha's early life could be a model for many people today. Think of the last time you were in a supermarket. Did you really think about how many things were in it? Were you aware that you, or at least your family, could probably buy

almost anything in that supermarket? Did it occur to you that for some people in today's world, being in a place like that and able to buy more or less whatever you wanted would be like paradise? Or did you just moan about the length of the checkout queues? Siddartha had everything he wanted until he realised that it was just a fairy tale illusion and he wanted Reality. For Buddhists, is that what being human is all about? Trying to get at what's real? Isn't that itself a desire? (And where does that leave the Third Noble Truth?)

Humans are, as far as we know, unique in that we have a sense of past, present and future. We can hope for things and work towards them. Maybe this ability is both our prize and our curse. Some people think that humans are more discontented now than ever before because it's so easy for us to see what we haven't got (and there's more for us to want, in material terms). Maybe this wanting and discontent blinds us to what we do have. Is it true that wanting things is like a ball and chain, which cling on to us and hold us back? For many people, life is good; so why then do so many people still seem unhappy? Buddhism teaches us that unhappiness arises because our cravings can't be satisfied, and so we need to stop craving. Once we have done that we'll have attained the state of Nibbana, complete non-attachment. At that point we will be all that we can be and no longer chained to desire. Then we will be truly human. But there's more. Before we can progress towards Nibbana, we need to open our eyes and wake up to the truth, which Buddhists describe as the Three Marks of Existence.

Activities

Knowledge, Understanding, Evaluation

1 How did Kisagotami get the answer to her request?

2 Do you think this answer was a satisfactory one? Explain your answer.

3 Do you think awareness that everyone suffers would help someone who was suffering?

4 In what ways was this the right way for the Buddha to help Kisagotami?

5 Why did Suddhodana keep Siddartha in the palace in the way he did?

6 Do you think Suddhodana was wise or silly for doing this?

7 How did Siddartha's life change completely?

8 Why can't wealth and power fight old age, sickness and death?

9 Was Siddartha right to leave his family? What about his responsibilities to his wife and family?

10 How might a Buddhist understand the meaning of the Mara story?

11 Do you believe in a Mara figure in the world today?

12 Do you think it would matter to Buddhists whether the story of Buddha's Enlightenment was literally true or not? Explain your answer.

13 In your own words, summarise the Four Noble Truths.

14 State six examples of Dukkha people might experience in the 21st century.

15 How does Tanha lead to Dukkha?

16 Explain what is meant by 'trying to detach yourself from things'.

17 Some people think this being detached is just sticking your head in the sand. What do you think?

18 How can Buddhists stop desire?

19 What kinds of things do people crave in today's world?

20 Do you think people could ever stop craving things?

Practical Activities

1 Make up a drama based on the story of the four sights. You could perform this for local primary children. Alternatively you could watch the film *Little Buddha*, then design your own storyboard for your own film of the Buddha's early life.

2 Turn the story of Kisagotami into a poem or words for a song. If you are musical you could also write the tune.

3 Create artwork to illustrate the first two Noble Truths. Try to use a variety of media. Use newspaper collages or draw more personal illustrations.

4 Buddhists believe in detaching themselves from the things of the world. Make a list of 'things you are attached to'. Which ones would be the most difficult to detach yourself from? Why? What benefits might you gain from doing so? Discuss in class and note down responses.

Unit Assessment Question

Int 1 How did the Buddha's response to Kisagotami help her? *(3)*

Int 2 What do Buddhists understand by Tanha? *(4)*

Higher

Explain what a Buddhist means by Dukkha. *(4)*

Sample Exam Question

Int 1 Which of the Four Noble Truths does the story of Kisagotami explain? *(4AE)*

Int 2 Why did what the Buddha saw in the village change him? *(4AE)*

Higher

How does Tanha lead to Dukkha? *(2KU, 2AE)*

Homework

Discuss the following question with a range of adults to compare their views with the views of people your age: 'As you get older, do you get more or less attached to certain things, or does it just stay the same?'

Personal Reflection

Buddhists believe that desire causes trouble. Are your desires causing trouble?

The Three Marks of Existence

The tale of Billy Glumsden

Poor old Billy Glumsden was full of gloom and woe
He brought a frown to every face wherever he did go
For all young Billy did all day was mump and gripe and moan
When people saw him coming they let out a doleful groan
('Oh no here's misery guts – run!')

It started in his RE class when he heard about Dukkha
'It fits, it's right, I understand. . . it's all clear now, aha!'
'Dukkha is suffering' his RE teacher howled
'It's everywhere, in everything – it's unavoidable' he scowled

Billy had been having quite a nice day until that
But now the weight of Dukkha made him feel like such a prat
For life was full of misery, suffering and despair
Illness, death, old age – losing all your hair

But worse than that it wasn't just these horrors from outside
There was a bit of Dukkha from which nobody could hide

For when you wish for something you cause yourself such pain –
The anguish of the hoping for the things you'll never gain

No matter what it is it's always just beyond your reach
A brand new toy, a new girlfriend or even just a peach
For even when you get it, you're still not satisfied
Cos now you will want something else and to that wish you're tied

On and on and on it goes, the never ending need
Desire, longing, lust for things – eternal shameless greed
It clings to you and drags you down and never goes away
So Dukkha caused young Billy to be moody every day

The worst thing is that Billy could have saved himself this sorrow
After learning of Dukkha said he, 'I'll see my guidance teacher tomorrow'
And so he did, he made a case and dropped out of RE
And sat and learned of wars and death in jolly History

Had Billy stayed and heard part two of the Dukkha story
He might have learned that it's not all doom, gloom and gory
For Buddhists don't sit around all day and think about what's bad
They smile and laugh, are cheery souls and generally glad...

That the Buddha had an answer to Dukkha

The Three Marks of Existence

Buddhists believe we need to become aware of the truth of our Reality, which they describe as the Three Marks of Existence:

◆ Mark 1: Dukkha

◆ Mark 2: Anatta

◆ Mark 3: Anicca.

Mark 1 – Dukkha: Can't live with it, can't live without it

Dukkha is pretty much anything grim – whether it comes from outside of you or from within you. Throwing up is Dukkha (inside and out, literally), but being afraid of throwing up is also Dukkha, as is the realisation that once it's over it might just happen all over again. Dukkha really means the things in life which are unsatisfactory. This means the things you can't have and the things you don't want as well as the things you can have and the things you do want, because it's not about *things*. It's about how you understand those things. Realising that life is basically unfulfilling is when you begin understanding Dukkha. Nothing ever stays the same and because of this, nothing – whether good or bad – will ever be the same twice. This means that unless you live moment to moment you're

THE HUMAN CONDITION

always going to be stuck in a cosmic mouse-wheel which makes you think that things will be better if only you could get to the end of where you think this mouse-wheel journey seems to be taking you. Think of the not terribly clever person who, when falling from a high building, is heard to mutter repeatedly, 'so far so good, so far so good'.

Now one of the biggest problems with Dukkha is that because there is no you (did that just say there is no you?), you can't achieve your desires (if there's no you, who's reading this?), and so you (who's that then?) suffer and cause yourself suffering.

Read the last paragraph again and see if you can make sense of it. This is one of the trickiest concepts in Buddhism and it comes down to the idea of the five skhandas, which should help you start to make sense of things.

Dukkha and 'suffering'

Of course for the vast majority of us, all is **not** suffering. If we are fortunate, we may often experience times when we are not suffering or we have happiness in our lives. This is where the use of 'suffering' as a translation for dukkha is too narrow, for dukkha means the frustration arising from blindly attaching to inherently unstable, undependable, imperfect conditions. So even a happy time can fool us into believing it will last and lead to anguish and frustration when the happy conditions change.

Source: www.buddhacommunity.org/eightfold.htm

Talk Point

9

Do you think life is full of suffering? Does everything good always have a downside?

Time Out

5

Think about what you think makes you you. What would have to change before you wouldn't think of yourself being you any more? Your appearance? Your personality? Compare ideas in class. Think about the implications of face/heart/brain transplants.

The five changing states of being: the five skhandas

In Buddhist teaching, everyone is made up of five factors – the five skhandas. When you begin to explore these states of being, what makes you you becomes a little less clear than it had seemed. The five skhandas cover aspects of our physical and non-physical being.

1 Rupa: the physical body

The physical body is pretty solid. There's no denying that it is real. But think about what's happening to you right now. You seem pretty solid and unchanging. But that's just an illusion. If you look back at photos of yourself in the past you'll see a different you. It is obvious your body has changed over time. But it is also changing right now. The last thing you ate is slowly changing into parts of you – maybe your hair or new blood cells or another annoying spot on your face. As you eat and grow and each tiny part of you changes, you change from one you into another you. And you never stop physically changing. Rub your nose right now – you've just altered your physical self forever. Some of the skin cells on your nose have come off and are now lying on your desk. You're different and that skin isn't you any more. This process of constant change happens right from the moment of birth until death. Even then, if you're buried, it continues as your physical self decays. But are you more than just the *physical* you?

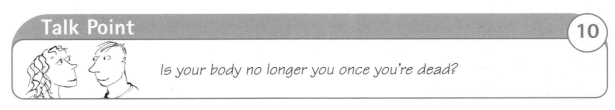

Talk Point   10

Is your body no longer you once you're dead?

2 Vedana: sensations and feelings

As you sit there you're also being assaulted by all sorts of sensations. There are the sensory ones like the sights, smells and sounds in your classroom. You see, you hear, you smell, you taste, you feel. These sensations change minute by minute, second by second. How much of them becomes a part of you? Test yourself. What was the first thing you heard as you walked into the class this period? The first smell? The first sight? Or what about what's on the wall behind you (don't turn around)? These sensations can affect the way you behave and how you understand things. They can also alter your feelings. But your feelings themselves are constantly changing. Maybe you started this RMPS class bored, but maybe now you're not. Maybe you're feeling happy because it's Friday or because you're having your favourite meal for dinner tonight. How you understand the world affects the *way* you are, and so it changes *what* you are (your personal characteristics).

THE HUMAN CONDITION

3 Sankhara: character traits – likes and dislikes

These are always changing too – especially at your age! Your parents are probably used to hearing you say things like, 'Well I don't like that today, right!' (usually when they've just gone to a great deal of trouble to make you your 'favourite' meal). All through your teenage years you try out new looks and new styles, new ways of being you. But it doesn't stop there; adults also try new things to see if they 'fit' the way they want to be. We like people to be consistent and not 'changeable'. But humans just are changeable – there's no way out of it. If you are what you like or are how you behave, then you've probably already been at least ten people today.

Time Out
6

What would you describe as your personality? How much has it changed in the last few years? Is it entirely under your control?

4 Sanna: cognitions

Things you know change too. You have already experienced being a baby in a pram but do you remember it? If you don't, was it really you? How can you really be sure? Do you consciously respond to everything you see or hear? Do you have to? Remember when you were (much) younger and you had to do a punishment exercise; after a few lines, you probably weren't really thinking about what you were doing. Was the person writing those lines still you? If you forgot everything that had ever happened to you, would you still be you? (Keep in mind that we've established that you're not the *physical* or the *personality* you. What is you? What is real?)

5 Vinnana: consciousness

Like many, when defending your belief in your own existence, you probably fall back on the idea of consciousness. You are aware of being you so … you are you. But what about when you're asleep? For many hours every day 'you' are no longer conscious that 'you' exist – so do you? What if you lost all your memories and your understanding of being you? Would you still be you? What about when you're unconscious? Is that still you in the proper sense of the word? Is there a proper sense of the word *you*?

Talk Point

Is the sleeping you actually still you?

(11)

Lots of books about Buddhism say that the five skhandas aren't the point. It's not what the Buddha said about them, but what he didn't say about them. And what he didn't say was that anyone has a soul or a spirit. We are constantly changing entities. There's nothing about us that stays the same. Thinking that there is some unchanging element in us becomes part of the problem of Dukkha (because it is this sense of an unchanging 'you' that has attachment to things) and is therefore the cause of suffering and its consequences.

The fleeting nature of you

The so-called being is like a flash of lightning that is resolved into a succession of sparks that follow upon one another with such rapidity that the human retina cannot perceive them separately, nor can the uninstructed conceive of such succession of separate sparks.

Source: www.buddhanet.net/nutshell09.htm

Mark 2 – Anatta: Soul-lessness

Because everything is changing all the time, there is no you. This is really what separated (and still separates) Buddhism from most other religions. Hindus believe in a soul called the *atman* – something which is uniquely you and survives beyond physical death. Buddhists believe that the whole idea that there's a 'you' is just a troublesome illusion. Not only that, it's something which makes 'you' attach yourself to things; hope, fear, desire and everything else which causes Dukkha and of which Dukkha is the result. So, for Buddhists, there is no such thing as the self. Now you could be rather sad about this, or you could look at it differently. If there's no self, then there's no need to be selfish. In fact, if you regard you and everything else as being nothing more than constantly changing, interconnected bundles of skhandas, then perhaps you'll be more interested in how 'you' (or your five skhandas) interact with others. If you no longer have a self, then perhaps you'll really begin to live in a selfless way – in every sense of the word. So for Buddhists, the idea of Anatta (not having a soul) is a central one.

One aspect of Buddhism which some people find difficult to understand is the idea of rebirth. How can you be reborn if there's no such thing as *you*? The Buddhist answer to this problem is quite straightforward: as your skhandas change constantly throughout life they set up patterns, and these patterns lead on to another rebirth and decide the nature of that rebirth. It is simple cause and effect. If you push a door open, it opens in a certain way. If you push it twice as

THE HUMAN CONDITION

hard, it opens in a different way. One causes the other. So your skhandas 'set up' a new pattern for a new being in the next life. But is this new being you? Yes . . . and no. The Buddha's answer to this question probably wouldn't go down too well in your RMPS class. He said that we shouldn't bother about questions like 'Do I exist after death?' Instead, he said we should spend our time trying to stop craving and in so doing find Nibbana.

Most Buddhists still talk about 'me', 'I', 'you' and 'myself'. So what's going on? Although there is no such thing as self in Buddhism, avoiding the use of 'I', 'you' and 'me' would make normal conversation and functioning very difficult (not to mention troublesome because you could always claim that 'you' can't be found guilty of anything since 'you' can't do anything since there's no 'you'). So Buddhists say that what we call ourselves is just a handy label for the state a particular set of skhandas is in at the moment.

How understanding helps us see clearly

Suppose we are walking down a country road at night. We look down at the ground and suddenly we see a snake and become frightened. Then we turn our flashlight [torch] on it. We look again and we see that there is only a rope, no snake. The rope was there all along, never a snake, but the rope appeared to us to be a snake because our sight was obscured by the darkness, because we did not focus our light on it. As a result of seeing a snake we became filled with fear and worry. When we found that it was only a rope, the appearance of the snake dissolved. We can compare the snake to the idea of self or ego, the flashlight to wisdom, and the rope to the complex of five aggregates [skandhas].

Source: www.beyondthenet.net/dhamma/ropeSnake.htm

Talk Point

(12)

Buddhists believe that 'little deaths' happen from moment to moment. You're constantly setting the pattern for the next rebirth (both minor rebirths – day to day – and major rebirth – at the end of this physical life). What pattern is your lifestyle setting up right now?

Mark 3 – Anicca: Impermanence

Not only is there no you, there's no real anything. Everything changes from one second to the next. What looks permanent is just an illusion. Even a mountain, which probably doesn't look all that different from afar year after year, is constantly changing, eroding away and changing shape ever so slowly. Even the Earth you live on is slowly changing and moving around; you only notice changes when something major happens, like an earthquake. Nothing stays the same. We only think it does, and this thinking leads to yet more Dukkha. (Maybe Billy Glumsden had a point.)

Because we're living a lie by thinking things are unchanging, we cause ourselves unhappiness. You can demonstrate this simply by going on holiday to the same place two or three years in a row. It might be better or worse each time, but it will always be different. We'd like it to be the same (especially if we have fond memories of it) but it just isn't. Things which we think are never going to change do change after a time. New teachers in school, new friends, your favourite shops closing and being replaced with boring shops, old venues being updated to become more exciting. It's all constantly on the move and always will be. We fool ourselves into thinking things stay the same – some people do this to try to keep themselves happy – and in doing so we're doomed to failure. Eventually we'll come to realise the truth that is Dukkha. We'll be shocked by the misery and suffering we're now aware of. On the other hand, maybe we won't realise that everything's changing. But unfortunately, in Buddhist teaching, that's no better because then our misery is even worse, because we don't even see it! Anicca is the term used by Buddhists to describe both this state of impermanence and our lack of awareness of it, and it is another central issue in Buddhist teaching.

On impermanence

Impermanence (anicca) is, of course, the essential fact which must be first experienced and understood by practice. Mere book-knowledge of the Buddha-Dhamma will not be enough for the correct understanding of anicca because the experiential aspect will be missing. It is only through experiential understanding of the nature of anicca as an ever-changing process within yourself that you can understand anicca in the way the Buddha would like you to understand it.

Source: www.pariyatti.com/ebd1.phtml

THE HUMAN CONDITION

Time Out 7

How might knowing that nothing is real affect your behaviour, whether good or bad?

Giving Billy Glumsden some hope

After what you've just read, you're probably thinking that Billy Glumsden was quite right to be so miserable. Yet, why aren't all Buddhists terribly depressed and utterly miserable? It's simple. Buddhists believe that there's nothing we can do about the fact that we have no self and that nothing is permanent. But once we are aware of that, then the gloom it would otherwise cast over our lives is gone. If we realise and accept that there's no self and that nothing stays the same, then it has absolutely no power over us. How could it? There's nothing for it to have power over – it can't fuel the flames of suffering and rebirth. So what do we do? Again, the answer is quite simple. Treat happiness and sadness in the same way, because both are illusions and an illusion isn't real and what isn't real can't make you sad. But knowing that it isn't real can make you happy. See, Billy should have stayed in RMPS.

Activities

Knowledge, Understanding, Evaluation

1 Why was Billy Glumsden glum? Why shouldn't he have been?

2 What is Dukkha? Give two examples from your own personal experience.

3 Is Dukkha the cause or the effect of suffering? Explain.

4 If the physical you is always changing, is there a physical you?

5 Is a feeling part of you?

6 Give an example of some of your Sankhara.

7 Can you only remember what really happened? (Or can you have very clear memories of things which never happened at all?)

8 Do you have to be conscious to be alive?

9 Explain what Buddhists mean by Anatta.

10 What do Buddhists believe goes on to the next rebirth?

11 How does the story about the rope and the snake explain the skhandas?

12 Why is Anicca likely to make us feel sad?

13 How can Buddhists still live quite happily even though they understand the Three Marks of Existence?

Practical Activities

1 Use what you have learned in this section to write a poem where Billy Glumsden comes back to RMPS and gets some help for his misery about Dukkha.

2 Use a variety of artistic media to illustrate the ideas of Dukkha, Anatta and Anicca. This could involve music, drama, art, photography etc.

3 Design a collage to represent the five skhandas.

4 Chart the changes you have gone through in life so far. Group them using the five skhandas: physical, emotional, personality, knowledge, consciousness.

5 Design a board game which explains to non-Buddhists what you have learned in this section, but make it fun – no misery allowed!

Unit Assessment Question

Int 1 What is the First Noble Truth?   *(3)*

Int 2 'The idea of Anicca is just depressing.' Would a Buddhist agree? Give reasons for your answer. *(6)*

Higher

Choose two of the five skhandas. Explain what Buddhism teaches about them.   *(6)*

Sample Exam Question

Int 1 According to Buddhists, why do living things suffer?   *(4KU)*

Int 2 Explain Buddhist beliefs about Anatta.   *(6KU)*

Higher

According to Buddhists, what is reborn after you die?   *(4KU, 4AE)*

Homework

Buddhists believe that your next rebirth is based on the patterns in life which you set up during this lifetime. Write your own views about what you might have to do in this lifetime to ensure a better rebirth next time. Ask two other people for their views and note down what they think. Are there any common ideas?

Personal Reflection

Does the fact that you know you will one day grow old and die affect how you live your life now?

Samsara, the Wheel of Life, the Three Root Poisons and Tanha

The wheel of Samsara

The wheel of Samsara (bhavacakra) – also called the wheel of life – was not the Buddha's idea. It already existed in the Hindu faith, where it was called the Cycle of Existence or the Path of Transmigration. It has been depicted in art through time as a way of helping people understand the idea of rebirth. Remember that Buddhists believe that nothing stays the same – everything is constantly changing – even life and death itself. Buddhists also believe that the patterns you set up in this life are the cause of the next rebirth. This is called **dependent origination**. All this means is that the origins of the next rebirth are dependent upon the life lived in the previous rebirth and so on, endlessly. By simple cause and effect, the pattern set up in the previous rebirth sets up the next pattern. Some rebirths are a bit more unlucky than others – for various, fairly obvious, reasons.

So what is the wheel showing us? What does it all mean? There are four circles shown in the wheel, each representing different aspects of this constant cycle of rebirth. Let's look at these different circles, starting at the very centre.

The three things in the middle – the pig, snake and rooster – are eating each other. Taken literally, this shows that everything depends on everything else for existence – even the strictest vegetarians still have to eat things which were once living. Symbolically, these animals represent the Three Root Poisons (pig – greed; snake – hatred; rooster – delusion) and how these feed off each other. (The Three Root Poisons are covered in more detail later in this section.)

wrong pig = ignorance/ delusion and rooster = greed.

Moving outwards to the next circle, there are some images showing the rebirth of one being through six existences. Three good existences are shown on the left while three evil existences are shown on the right.

Moving outwards again to the third circle, there are the realms through which rebirth can move. Starting at the bottom there's Hell. There are quite a few hells and you don't stay there forever. Once you've paid the debt of the bad actions which caused you to be reborn in hell, you can move on. Next, there's the

animal realm. Animals, poor things, don't have much choice about how they live their life and it's difficult for them to live good lives so that they can improve and achieve a better rebirth. But it can be done, it just takes longer. There is also the realm of ghosts. These are beings who are so attached to earthly life that they find it hard to let go and move on. Desire has got them in its grip. Next, there is the realm of the Titans. These are basically bloodthirsty, violent demi-gods who think they'll become happy by exercising their filthy little aggressive habits, but they don't. Next, there is the human realm, which is not a bad place to be. Here, you can make choices and have some control over the patterns you set up for the next rebirth. (So make the most of it!) Finally, there is the realm of Heaven, in which there are various heavens. The heavens vary in 'style' and importance, from a nice but small riverside flat to a rolling mansion with acres of ground … in a manner of speaking. However, in Buddhism, reaching Heaven isn't the end goal; once you're there you might start to become a bit complacent or you might want so much to stay there that you become attached and greedy for more. All of this means that, unless you are careful, you can slip back down from the heavens through the various realms all over again!

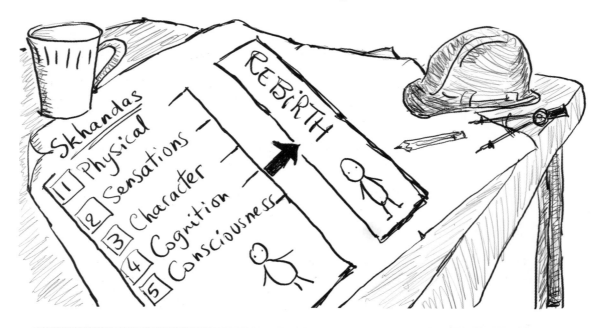

Time Out

8

How does this Buddhist view of life and death/heaven and hell differ from other religions you might have studied? Is it a model you like better than others?

Twelve stages of dependent origination

The outer rim of the circle shows the twelve stages of dependent origination (nidanas). This gives some idea about how things link to each other as cause and effect.

1 Ignorance: a man who can't see might bump into things; ignorance of what's real makes us stumble about in the darkness, not seeing anything for what it is.

2 Kammic formation: what you do affects how you act and what you do; once you use your senses, for example seeing, you can make things, and as you try to get things clear your actions have causes and make new things (not always pots).

3 Consciousness: jumpy monkey; up and down it restlessly scampers, uncontrolled, never sitting still (just like life!).

4 Mind and matter: man and woman (mind) in a rowing boat (matter or form); ideas become forms and start to interact with the real world. Some Buddhists see this as the patterns of the previous life rowing towards joining the new being as it is conceived in the womb.

5 Empty house: the empty body and the senses; waiting to be furnished by the new pattern which the rebirth has set up.

6 Contact: man and woman embracing; arising from consciousness of being male and female, the senses and the wants meet, resulting in emotions and defilements, and the contact between perception and reality begins.

7 Feeling: man with arrow in eye; the emotions and feeling now stirred by sensory experience and contact can be painful or pleasurable, and they blind you (again) to the reality of things.

8 Craving: man drinking alcohol; the feelings and desires take hold and you want more and more of them (addictions starting).

9 Grasping: monkey snatching fruit; just as the monkey grasps the fruit and won't let go, so desires cling to you and you to them – attachment to things takes hold.

10 Becoming: pregnant woman; all this leads to another rebirth and the creation of a thing which is dependent upon everything that has gone before.

11 Rebirth: woman giving birth; the new life which arises is a product of the patterns set up to this point.

12 Old age and death: dead body being carried; death comes 'soon' afterwards (even though you might think 70 years or so is a long time off).

And the whole cycle begins all over again.

> ## Cause and effect
>
> It is the everlasting and unchanging rule of this world that everything is caused by a series of causes and conditions and everything disappears by the same rule; everything changes, nothing remains constant.
>
> Some say everything has been decided by destiny . . . some say that everything is created by God . . . some say that everything happens by chance . . .
>
> In fact, these three conceptions . . . are all wrong: everything is a succession of appearances whose source is the accumulation of causes and conditions.

Source: The Teaching of Buddha, by Bukkyo Dendo Kyokai

A confused picture?

Now maybe you're a little confused – what's all this about demi-gods, hells and heavens? If you thought Buddhism didn't have gods and everything was an illusion anyway, you'd be right – sort of. Different Buddhists have different views about these things, and at this RMPS level you don't need to know the intricate reasons behind these differences. The most straightforward explanation is that, as the teaching of the Buddha was understood and developed, sometimes it got mixed together with local beliefs and even superstitions. This means that modern Buddhism is often a tricky combination of the teachings of the Buddha and many other ideas and beliefs borrowed from Hinduism or other local religions where Buddhism took hold. For the purposes of this course, you just need to know that this wheel of life or cycle of Samsara is a pictorial representation of the idea that one thing leads inevitably to another, and that everything is constantly in motion. How one thing is in a particular stage of rebirth leads on to how the next rebirth is set up. You need to build up all the right bits to make up the required pattern next time. Think of dependent origination as like having a Lego set: you can only build with what you have. If you don't have the right bricks you can't build the fancy house you want – you can only make what the bricks you actually have allow. Remember that Buddhists aren't reincarnated (because there would have to be a 'you' to be reincarnated); instead, they are reborn (or rather the pattern they have set up in this life leads to a rebirth in the next). Each new rebirth is conditioned by the previous one.

The wheel of fortune – it's your choice

Imagine carrying out a survey. You ask 20 people these three questions:

◆ Is it right to kill?

◆ Is it right to take what is not yours?

◆ Is it right to look after your children?

Now, for the sake of argument, imagine you could ask the same questions of some animals, for example, lions, gorillas and budgerigars. What answers (assuming they could all understand and answer the question) would each give to these questions?

Talk Point ⑬

What answers do you think the humans and the animals would give? How might they be different? What do these differences tell us about their moral views?

Given the imaginary nature of such a survey, there's no obvious answer. It's probably true that the human answers would come in a greater variety of forms. Most of the animal answers would probably concern personal survival and ensuring that the species continues. The human answers would probably take into account things like power, responsibility, selfishness and selflessness. The humans would be better placed to think of the consequences of choices and how different choices would lead to possibly different outcomes.

In Buddhism, the fact that humans can make moral choices is very important. (It's also why you can be stuck in the animal realm for quite a long time.) If everything is changing and rebirth is moment to moment based on the pattern you set up (in this and in previous rebirths), then how you set up that pattern is by making choices in life. These can be **active** choices, made by choosing to do option X instead of Y, or they can be **passive** choices, made by not doing anything at all, or simply avoiding making choices (which is still a choice). But how do we decide what is good or bad?

For Buddhists, intention is very important. What you mean to happen when you make a choice is a major factor in making the choice good or bad. Actions can be classed according to two opposing sets of motivations. Making a moral choice based on the outcome you want (partly) decides if it's good or bad:

- good actions are based on these intentions: non-attachment; kindness; understanding

- bad actions are based on these intentions: attachment; nastiness; ignorance.

Good intentions should lead to good actions or neither is really all that good! Humans, as far as we know, are capable of making conscious ethical choices. The choices we make are the causes of the effects that follow. It's not good or bad luck; think of it as being like a wheel of fortune. When someone spins the arrow on the wheel of fortune, it isn't by chance that it stops in a particular place; rather, it is the consequence of how hard the person pushed the arrow, how well-oiled the spinning mechanism is, and so on. (A clever physicist could probably work out how to make the arrow stop at every point on the wheel of fortune!) The Samsaric wheel of life is similar. Your progress through it, fast or slow, up or down, depends upon the choices you make and the actions you take – simple cause and effect. If your decisions are motivated by nastiness then you're likely to move down, but if they are based on kindness then you're likely to move up. It's not really that difficult.

Time Out 9

What makes a choice good or bad? What you mean to happen or what actually happens? Can you have good intentions that lead to bad consequences? Have you therefore done something bad?

The Three Root Poisons

A cautionary tale

Once upon a time there were three little pigs. They left home and decided to build their own houses. They were always on the lookout for the big bad wolf who, as you shall see, had rather an easy time of it, despite some bad press. He was a wolf after all, what did you expect him to eat? Tofu? Besides, as you'll see, these three particular little pigs won't deserve much of your sympathy.

The first little pig was called Greedy Snorks. Every penny he made went into getting hold of straw to build his house. He didn't give to charity or pay his

taxes. He just bought more straw. But he held on to the straw so long that it grew mouldy. Other people offered to help him out and replace his straw with new stuff (who knows what they were going to do with tired old straw), but he'd have none of it. It was his and he was keeping it all. And so he built his house of mouldy straw. Along came the wolf and tried to blow his house down. But first he had a gentle cough to clear his throat. By this time the straw was so mouldy it just crumbled at this weak little cough and Greedy Snorks became meal number one.

The second pig was Hateful Snorks. He didn't bother working – he just stole. Sticks mostly. He even stole sticks from an old lady's winter supplies and she had a pretty cold time that year. He stole sticks from children who were playing with them, and he stole sticks which were holding up people's plants and their plants collapsed and died. With all these sticks he built himself a house. Along came the wolf and tried to blow his house down, but he couldn't. That is, until all the people who'd had sticks nicked by Hateful Snorks came along to help the wolf and together they blew up Hateful Snorks' house. He became meal number two.

Finally there was Deluded Snorks. He lived in his own wee fantasy world. Now he did work and decided to build his house of bricks. One day a man came along selling lovely polystyrene bricks. They looked just like the real thing, but were much cheaper and looked great. Deluded Snorks bought loads of them thinking that everyone would be impressed with his grand brick house – only he would know it was polystyrene. Who was he trying to kid? Along came the wolf, threatening to blow Deluded Snorks' house down. Deluded Snorks had by now come to believe his own lie, and laughed at the wolf ('blow down a house of bricks?!'). Of course the wolf blew and found that the polystyrene bricks flew off in all directions. Meal number three. The wolf discovered that the world was full of greedy, hateful and deluded little pigs. So he lived happily ever after...

These poor little pigs represent the Buddhist idea of the Three Root Poisons. Of course, being pigs they can't (as far as we know) make *conscious ethical choices* – only humans can do this. This ability of people to freely choose right or wrong is central to Buddhism – unless we are free to act we can't be thought of as being responsible for our own actions. Buddhists believe that we *can* choose and so we *have* to accept the consequences of our choices. But back to the three pigs: as greed, hatred and delusion, they represent the heart of the desire which causes you to be caught up in the endless cycle of Samsara or rebirth. It is these Root Poisons which constantly set up the pattern for the next rebirth (in this life or the next). Now, greed, hatred and delusion have pretty obvious meanings, but in Buddhism there are various levels or degrees of each. For example, outright hatred obviously isn't going to make you a better person, but there are 'smaller', more subtle forms of hatred which are damaging too and contribute to a harmful pattern being set up. The Dhammasangani, the first book of the Abhidhamma Pitaka, gives some other examples of these Three Root Poisons, which should give you a clearer idea about what they're all about.

Greed

Obviously this includes 'I want, I want, it's all mine'. But it is also:

◆ wishing – not being happy with what you have and wanting more

◆ passion – being so attached to something that other things are put into second place (might even be watching football!)

◆ ambition or desiring attention – it could be starring on 'Big Brother' or just in the chorus of the school musical.

Greed is a problem because it is about being so attached to things that you can't think of anything else. It's also the idea that things can satisfy you, whether they are material things or feelings and sensations. Watching your football team win is enjoyable, but the happy feeling only lasts a short while, and leaves you greedy for another win. No matter how many times your team win, you always want more. Greed also puts your wants before anyone else's and that's obviously a problem!

Hatred

Now you can hate a person or a spider, and hatred can lead to anything from gossiping behind someone's back to stamping on poor defenceless little spiders. Hatred is also:

◆ dislike – this is not as strong as hating but it is still thinking badly or negatively about something

◆ resentment – this is feeling hard done by or that an injustice has taken place and you're the victim

◆ irritability – the feeling of being annoyed by something which could lead to you reacting badly to it.

Hatred in its strongest form is not good – it leads to conflict, wars, death and destruction, but the more subtle forms are bad too. Like the 'lesser' forms of greed, these little hatreds lead you to thinking that you're better than the object of your 'hatred' and so devalue the other person (or thing) and make you feel that you're more than you are. Hatred and greed are both forms of fooling yourself into becoming too attached to your own self-importance at the expense of other things.

Delusion

Buddhism teaches that everything is an illusion – nothing stays the same. Delusion is when we fool ourselves (either on purpose or unthinkingly) that things are what we *think* they are rather than what they *are*. Delusion is also:

◆ confusion – most of us in the Western world now suffer from 'options overload' – we have too many choices. Yet, how many times have you complained that you 'have nothing to do'? And how does this match up with the variety of options actually available to you? (Think about the number of sports and hobby clubs in your area, how many TV stations there are to watch or books to read, activities to do on computers, and so on.) Things can *feel* unsatisfactory because there's so much to choose from and you're confused about where satisfaction can obtained.

◆ prejudice – again, this is based on thinking that you're better than someone else. Even telling a slightly 'off colour' joke deludes you (and your audience) into thinking that you're better than the subject of your joke.

◆ dogmatism – this is the 'I'm right and you're wrong' approach to life. People who are dogmatic about anything (football, music, religion) delude themselves and become attached to their own delusion rather than reality. What might seem 'obvious' is just polystyrene bricks.

Delusion is a particular problem because it really sums up the Second Noble Truth – that suffering is caused by desire.

How the Three Root Poisons taint us

Greed, hatred, and delusion are deeply embedded in the conditioning of our personalities. Our behavior is habitually influenced and tainted by these three poisons, these unwholesome roots buried deep into our mind. Burning within us as lust, craving, anger, resentment, and misunderstanding, these poisons lay to waste hearts, lives, hopes, and civilisations, driving us blind and thirsty through the seemingly endless round of birth and death (samsara). The Buddha describes these defilements as bonds, fetters, hindrances, and knots; the actual root cause of unwholesome kamma and the entire spectrum of human suffering.

Source: www.naljorprisondharmaservice.org/pdf/ThreePoisons.htm

Time Out   ⑩

Do a bit of self-examination. In your life, what evidence is there of you showing any of the Three Root Poisons? You might like to compare your views with others (or you might want to keep it to yourself).

Craving

All kinds of craving, if looked at carefully, turn out to be just different forms or manifestations of the underlying desire to perpetuate our existence. The great power of this force pushing for life does not just vanish at the time of death, but these urgings for renewed existence *(bhava sankharas)* become the cause of rebirth in the appropriate place.

Source: www.accesstoinsight.org/lib/authors/jootla/wheel301.html

Tanha

This is a small word for a big idea, and it covers much of what has already been described. The Three Root Poisons are all Tanha. The fact that we desire things is human nature, but it's not helpful in terms of our progression towards Nibbana. Our desires lead to hopes and expectations that our wishes will come true. Whether they do or not, they are still ultimately unsatisfactory. The happiness and contentment we thought they would bring either doesn't come at all or comes and then fades away, leaving us hungrier for more of the same (or a

better version of it). Tanha is desire that is either valued too highly or is directed wrongly. Tanha includes the expectation of sensory pleasures. But not all desires are necessarily Tanha; Buddhists use the word Chanda to describe positive desires such as wanting the best for others or desiring to be a better person. Regardless of its form, desire is the fuel which keeps the wheel of Samsara turning. Two of the Four Noble Truths use the word Tanha – it's therefore pretty central to Buddhist teaching.

Talk Point

(14)

Discuss what you think is Tanha and what is Chanda in your own life

We experience Tanha because we fail to realise that everything is impermanent. Wanting things is always bound to result in unhappiness because the 'reward' can only be temporary. If everything is changing then happiness can only be short-lived. If this is the case, then it's not satisfactory and this will lead us to seek new happiness. So, every little happiness is inevitably tied to a little sadness. We don't realise that things are impermanent because we are ignorant.

Avijja

The notion of Avijja – ignorance of the Reality of things – had been around in Hinduism before the Buddha. The Hindu god Shiva Nataraj is often portrayed as a dancer (Shiva keeps the universe in motion through the dance, which is a similar idea to the wheel of life). Shiva is often shown standing on a little creature which Hindus recognise as Avijja or ignorance. This isn't ignorance like burping loudly in class, but the proper sense of the word. The word Avijja means lack of knowledge or understanding of the true nature of the Reality of things.

THE HUMAN CONDITION

This is what ignorance means too. The word 'ignorance' comes from the Greek language and literally means 'without knowledge' (knowledge = *Gnosis*; note the similar sounds?). This lack of knowledge doesn't mean that you haven't learned enough facts or understood enough information; it means a lack of understanding of the way things *are*. For Buddhists, Avijja means fooling yourself into thinking that things are permanent when they're not. This ignorance leads to desire which leads to unhappiness which leads to desire which leads to unhappiness. Getting the cyclic nature of the teachings of Buddhism, yet?

What does this all mean for the Human Condition?

Ignorance, however, isn't just a misplaced belief in the permanence of things in this world. It leads to actions. We behave in certain ways because of what we believe. If we are ignorant of the true nature of things and their impermanence, then we will live in ways which result from this ignorance, with lives full of greed, hatred and delusion – the Three Root Poisons and all the things which hold us back in life (this life, as well as all the others that have been and are to come). You are where you are right now because of ignorance and the Tanha which it gives rise to. Your patterns have been set by the choices 'you' have made in this and previous rebirths. Life is unsatisfactory because we expect it to be one thing when it's actually another thing altogether. But before we can move on and do something about this unsatisfactoriness, we have to become aware of what we really are and what we're really aiming for. What, therefore, are life's goals?

Activities

Knowledge, Understanding, Evaluation

1 In your own words, describe the wheel of Samsara.

2 What is at the centre of the wheel? What do these represent?

3 What do Buddhists mean by dependent origination?

4 Describe one of the realms of existence in detail.

5 Is the wheel of Samsara a helpful image for Buddhists? Explain your answer.

6 How does the outer rim of the wheel show cause and effect?

7 According to Dendo Kyokai, what causes everything?

8 Could a gorilla be blamed for stealing a banana? Explain.

9 Why is the fact that humans can make moral choices important in Buddhism?

10 Is something right if you 'mean well'?

11 What is the moral in the story given here of the three little pigs?

12 Describe the Three Root Poisons and give an example of each from your own experience.

13 Do you think that the Three Root Poisons are avoidable?

14 What is delusion and why is it an important idea in Buddhism?

15 In what way can delusion be a 'fetter'?

16 Would you like to live forever? What would be good and bad about it? Do you think wanting to do this is really something which causes people problems?

17 What is Tanha?

18 Is Chanda as bad as Tanha? Explain your answer.

19 In what way is Anicca linked to Tanha?

20 What is Avijja?

21 Do you think that you suffer from Avijja? Explain your answer.

22 What problems can Avijja lead to?

Practical Activities

1 Make your own version of the wheel of Samsara, using a collage of images from newspapers and magazines, etc.

2 Illustrate the twelve stages of dependent origination.

3 Have a class debate on the topic 'Animals cannot be held responsible for their actions'.

4 Play a game of consequences. Think of two or three actions which might be the result of a moral decision. Think of all the possible consequences which might follow from these actions. Draw these as a flowchart or schematic diagram, using labels 'good', 'bad', 'intentions', 'outcomes' and so on.

5 Turn the slightly twisted version of the three pigs story into a short drama. You could act this out for younger classes in school (but don't upset them). You could include a narrator who explains the meaning of the story at the end.

6 Write a news report or a tabloid newspaper article on the Three Root Poisons.

Unit Assessment Question

Int 1 How does the wheel of life explain the idea of Samsara? (4)

Int 2 Explain one of the Three Root Poisons. (4)

Higher

'Tanha is caused by Avijja.' Would a Buddhist agree? (6)

Sample Exam Question

Int 1 Describe a realm of existence which you would find in an image of the wheel of life. *(4KU)*

Int 2 'We experience Tanha because we fail to realise that everything is a delusion.' How would a Buddhist explain this statement? *(4KU, 4AE)*

Higher

'Suffering comes from our failure to live in accordance with the knowledge that all things are impermanent.' Would a Buddhist agree? *(8AE)*

Homework

Write your own fairy tale which illustrates one of the ideas you have studied during this section.

Personal Reflection

Do any or all of the Three Root Poisons have a hold on you?

Textual Sources

As with all the texts in this course, you should read them in their original form. Remember to use the version of the Dhammapada which the SQA advises, but it's a good idea to look at other versions too. Sometimes the way something is translated in a different version might help you to understand it all better.

Dhammapada 147–156

Dhammapada text	Commentary
147 Behold this body – a painted image, a mass of heaped up sores, infirm, full of hankering – of which nothing is lasting or stable.	*Physical life is unsatisfactory and we are always wanting more – it's pointless to be like that because nothing stays the same.*
148 Fully worn out is this body, a nest of disease and fragile. This foul mass breaks up, for death is the end of life.	*The body is revolting and weak. It is constantly decomposing towards death.*
149 These dove-coloured bones are like gourds that lie scattered about in autumn. Having seen then, how can one seek delight?	*Gourds are part of the natural cycle of some plants – their falling to the ground is further evidence that things are always changing.*
150 This body is built of bones, plastered with flesh and blood; within are decay and death, pride and jealousy.	*Further reinforcement of the notion that the body is continuously decaying and heading towards death.*
151 Even gorgeous royal chariots wear out, and indeed this body wears out too. But the Dhamma of the Good does not age; thus the Good make it known to the good.	*The teaching of the Buddha offers some stability in an otherwise unstable and unsatisfactory life.*
152 The man of little learning grows old like a bull. He grows only in bulk, but his wisdom does not grow.	*Experience in life is meaningless unless you learn from it.*

153 Through many a birth in samsara have I wandered in vain, seeking the builder of this house (of life). Repeated birth is indeed suffering!	*Not that there's someone or something behind it all, but that there must be some rules governing all this rebirth and suffering – what could they be?*
154 O house-builder, you are seen! You will not build this house again. For your rafters are broken and your ridgepole shattered. My mind has reached the unconditioned: I have attained the destruction of craving.	*The house is your existence, it is built through craving. Its structures are built of passions and ignorance. Once you see these for the impostors they are, your 'house' or existence will cease to be.*
155 Those who in youth have not led the holy life, or have failed to acquire wealth, languish like old cranes in a pond without fish.	*Doesn't mean financial wealth, but instead a 'wealth' of understanding of the true nature of things, without which you will be weakened.*
156 Those who in youth have not led the holy life, or have failed to acquire wealth, lie sighing over the past, like worn out arrows shot from a bow.	*If you have lived in ignorance you will stay in ignorance. You will therefore be powerless to cause any changes to your continued existence.*

Dhammapada 334–342

Dhammapada text	Commentary
334 The craving of one given to heedless living grows like a creeper. Like the monkey seeking fruits in the forest, he leaps from life to life.	*Craving never ends – you try one thing, then another, always looking for a better sensation or a new experience. But there's no point – all are fruitless (pun intended).*
335 Whoever is overcome by this wretched and sticky craving, his sorrows grow like grass after the rains.	*Craving clings to you and feeds more craving. The more you get the more you want – a vicious circle.*
336 But whoever overcomes this wretched craving, so difficult to overcome, from him sorrows fall away like water from a lotus leaf.	*Lotus leaves sit on top of water and so are pretty waterproof. Water tends to fall on them and then run off without a trace – a good image for what would happen to existence if you could stop craving.*
337 Dig up the root of craving, like one in search of the fragrant root of the birana grass. Let not Mara crush you again and again as a flood crushes a reed.	*Get to the point of craving and stop it before it takes hold (like roots do for a plant). It won't be easy and you'll be constantly tempted to stray off the path – keep at it!*
338 Just as a tree, though cut down, sprouts up again if its roots remain uncut and firm, even so, until the craving that lies dormant is rooted out, suffering springs up again and again.	*You need to make sure that you give up every single tiny shred of craving – if you don't it will just take hold again like a weed and grow back.*

339 The misguided man in whom the thirty-six currents of craving strongly rush toward pleasurable objects, is swept away by the flood of his passionate thoughts.	*Craving can also build momentum and get you quite literally carried away. You think craving can be satisfied – it can't – you'll drown.*
340 Everywhere these currents flow, and the creeper sprouts and grows. Seeing that the creeper has sprung up, cut off its roots with wisdom.	*Temptations are everywhere and there's plenty for them to feed on. Ignorance feeds craving – banishing ignorance is the way to end craving.*
341 Flowing in and watered by craving, feelings of pleasure arise in beings. Bent on pleasures and seeking enjoyment, these men fall prey to death and decay.	*Don't be a slave to your desires. They'll kill you.*
342 Beset by craving, people run about like an entrapped hare. Therefore one who yearns to be passion-free should destroy his own craving.	*You may not even realise that craving has you in its grip – so it's best not to let it get hold of you in the first place.*

Textual work

The following is the kind of exam question on texts you may meet in your RMPS exam. **Remember**, there are no prescribed sources at **Intermediate 1**.

Read the following source, then answer all of the parts of the question (a)–(e). The number of marks available for each part is indicated; use them to help you answer the question.

Dhammapada 153

'Through many a birth in samsara have I wandered in vain, seeking the builder of this house (of life). Repeated birth is indeed suffering!'

(a) What is Samsara? *(4KU)*

(b) Why do Buddhists want to escape Samsara? *(2KU, 2AE)*

(c) According to Buddhism, what rules govern rebirth? *(6KU)*

(d) 'Suffering is central to Buddhism.' Would a Buddhist agree? *(8AE)*

(e) How can the Buddhist ensure that the 'house is not built again'? *(4KU)*

(26 marks)

Big Tam is in a football team. He's rubbish. But because he's Big Tam and bigger than everyone else, no one has the guts to tell him that he's rubbish. What's more, he's the goalie and so his team regularly lose by goals in double figures. Big Tam has no idea why his team loses every week. He is happy with his goal-keeping skills, even though his team keeps losing. Everyone thinks Big Tam needs to wake up to reality and to realise why his team loses every week. But how can they get him to understand it for himself?

What should they do about Big Tam? What should Big Tam do?

What are your aims in life? Do you have any? What is the point of your existence? Is there any? Does whether you have any aims or not affect how you live? What is real and what is unreal? Can we ever truly understand the meaning of life? Should we be trying to? How should we live our lives and what are we living them for?

Sitting in class right now you probably have some plans for the future, aiming for something. But what? And why? How important these goals are for you will affect most of the things you do. Are your goals realistic? What will you have to do to achieve them? Can you do it on your own? What if you have no goals? What kind of life might you lead? A different one?

Buddhists believe that there is a purpose to our existence, and that our life is for something. And what about the end of life? The inevitability of dying is something we all have in common. Is that it? Is there something which continues after death? If there is, is it 'you'? How does the life you have led affect what happens afterwards? Are things happening to you now because of the patterns you set up in previous lives?

Buddhists don't think that what happens 'after death' is the only issue. They believe that a new 'you' is created moment by moment, even in your 'current' life. This new you is based on the choices made by the previous you. In a way, Buddhists believe that you 'die' from moment to moment. So, how you live your life doesn't just affect what happens to you after your physical death – it's about the kind of person you are constantly recreating yourself as in this life.

Buddhists believe that we are all living in ignorance. The goal of life is to progress towards Enlightenment, a stage where we are no longer ignorant of the true nature of Reality. Then we will also be Enlightened beings. To reach this state of Enlightenment: that's what life is for.

If Big Tam became a Buddhist, he could enlighten himself about the reality of his goalie skills and he'd be a much happier person than he already is ... wouldn't he?

Getting into it

◆ What are your goals in life?

◆ Do you think life has a point?

◆ What do you believe happens after death?

◆ How does this affect how you think you should live your life?

◆ What kind of life should you live?

◆ How do your beliefs and actions affect your life?

◆ How much of your life should be about you and how much should it be about others?

◆ Do you think that you are living in ignorance?

◆ What are you aiming for in your life?

The Law of Kamma: Skilful and Unskilful Actions

The scene is the popular TV show 'Mastermind'. The big black chair sits ominously in the centre of the room, ready for the next victim. A Buddhist monk in flowing orange robes takes his seat and awaits his grilling...

HOST:	Your name.
BHIKKU:	Bhikku Amforashandi.
HOST:	And your specialist subject?
BHIKKU:	Desire.
HOST:	Bhikku Amforashandi, you have two minutes on the subject of desire starting now. According to the Second Noble Truth of Buddhism, What causes suffering?
BHIKKU:	Desire.
HOST:	Correct. What is the goal of the Buddhist?
BHIKKU:	To escape the wheel of Samsara and attain Enlightenment.
HOST:	Correct. Do you want to escape Samsara and attain Enlightenment?
BHIKKU:	(a little confused by this non-factual question...) Er ... yes.
HOST:	Correct. And does the fact that you want this mean that you desire it?
BHIKKU:	(shifts uncomfortably) Well ... yes, I suppose it does.
HOST:	Correct. So you desire Enlightenment?
BHIKKU:	Well, it's not really like that...
HOST:	I'll take that as a 'pass'. Do you do good things?
BHIKKU:	(very confused now) Well, yes, of course I do.
HOST:	And do you do these for yourself or for others?

THE GOALS

> BHIKKU: Well, a bit of both really. I want all beings to be happy.
> HOST: Correct. But you obviously desire this and when it happens you are happy?
> BHIKKU: Sorry, could you repeat the question?
> HOST: You desire happiness for others and this makes you feel good?
> BHIKKU: But both are illusions...
> HOST: But you want the illusion of happiness more than the illusion of misery?
> BHIKKU: I thought this was a quiz show?
> HOST: Is it right (bleeper). I've started, so I'll finish. Is it right to desire anything?
> BHIKKU: But it's all just cause and effect. The natural laws of Kamma.
> HOST: Thank you, Bhikku Amforashandi. You have scored five points, but I imagine that you never really wanted to win anyway did you? You may leave the chair.

Talk Point 15

From what you have learned about Buddhism so far, would it be wrong for a Buddhist to desire anything?

Desiring a goal?

The Second Noble Truth states that all suffering comes from desire. So should Buddhists desire anything? A goal is obviously something you want. If you want it, isn't that desire and won't it lead to suffering? That's a tricky question. There are obviously certain things in life you just have to do – like eating and sleeping. These are not goals – you don't desire to do them, they are just things you do which would make life pretty unpleasant if you didn't. Lack of sleep and food would lead to a very sleepy, grumpy you and wouldn't be much fun for those around you either. Buddhists would say that, like many things in our lives, attaining our goals is just another example of cause and effect. The trouble with cause and effect is that you can never be completely sure how they are linked. The film *The Butterfly Effect* is a very good example of this. In this film a time-travelling character keeps going back in time to put things right in the past. The trouble is that each time he does this, the effects of what he changes aren't what he'd planned. He often ends up making things worse. So does the idea of trying to achieve some kind of goal lead to good consequences or bad? It's hard to say, but for Buddhists the crucial point is the intention behind the action.

Time Out 11

Imagine you could go back in time and change the past. Should you do it?

The Law of Kamma

Remember the idea of dependent origination? This states that your present existence is shaped by the pattern of actions set up in previous existences. There was no God or gods weighing this up and deciding for you. It was just cause and effect. One thing leads to another, just as a falling ball is acted upon by the law of gravity. Therefore your actions are everything, and since your actions are tied to your beliefs, then what you think and what you do set up patterns for rebirth. This is the Law of Kamma. Kamma is like kicking a football. How fast and how far the ball travels depends on the force and angle of your kick. Where it moves depends on the direction in which you kicked it. It might even achieve a goal. The Law of Kamma says that throughout life your thoughts lead to actions which lead to consequences. The shape, direction and force of these thoughts and actions decide the consequences... they even decide if you're likely to achieve your goal or not.

For Buddhists, the Law of Kamma shows quite clearly that we are masters of our own lives. Things that happen to us happen because we have made it that way. They believe that everything that happens is the result of Kamma – in the form of good or bad luck – all of which you have brought upon yourself during one rebirth or another. For example, if you slice off your little finger while chopping a carrot then that isn't sheer 'bad luck' but rather is an event brought about in some way by the Kamma you have built up over time and you just have to accept it. Other Buddhists don't agree with this. They believe that Kamma is like a great universal lottery. Their view is that there are such things as genuine 'accidents' and such random events are not linked to Kamma. For these Buddhists, Kamma refers only to the choices we make in this life, in particular, the moral choices. The moral choices we make determine whether our Kamma is good or bad.

Talk Point 16

What was the last moral choice you made? Do you think it led to good or bad Kamma?

Kamma

Reduced to its most elementary meaning, kamma is action; it also refers to the fruits of action. It may be seen as the law of causation on a personal level, a combination of primary and secondary causes. In the case of a plant, for example, the seed is the primary cause and the rain, wind sunlight etc are the secondary causes. Similarly, every thought, utterance, and deed is a seed that ripens over time until, under suitable conditions, it comes to fruition as an event or circumstance.

Source: www.buddhanet.net

Intentions or consequences?

Whether intentions or consequences are more important when deciding the 'goodness' of an action is an issue not only for Buddhists but also for many other areas of RMPS study.

Mr Bungle, Mr Bongle and their good actions

Suppose there are two homeless people, Bert and Bart, sitting side by side outside a burger shop. Mr Bungle takes pity on Bert and gives him a few pounds. Mr Bongle does the same for Bart. Both Mr Bungle and Mr Bongle have done good things – yes? Both have done equally good things – yes? With his few pounds Bert goes and buys himself a sandwich. This gives him some energy and makes him feel good. He decides to be more positive about things and goes and gets himself a job which leads to him getting some qualifications. After many years he ends up as the Head Teacher of a large secondary school. And all of this happened because of those few pounds given by Mr Bungle. Bart, however, takes his few pounds, buys a bottle of cheap wine and gets drunk. While drunk he ends up in a fight with a policeman and is put in prison. Over many years he returns to this prison. And all of this happened because of those few pounds given by Mr Bongle.

Now we can't really blame Mr Bungle or Mr Bongle for the lives of Bert and Bart, but their decisions to lend a few pounds sparked off a chain of events which led to very different outcomes. So were their actions good or not?

Talk Point

17

It looks as if Mr Bungle has been a hero and Mr Bongle an idiot. Is that fair?

Philosophers disagree on whether the actions of Bongle and Bungle were good or not. Many argue that something is right or good because of the intention behind it, not because of the consequences which follow from it. Others say that you can't really separate the two that easily because sometimes someone does something very bad based on very good intentions. Buddhists believe that the

answer is something of a *mixture* of intentions and consequences. The Buddha explained that Kammic choices were like seeds. The seeds would grow and produce fruit according to the type of seed sown. The moral choices we make (cetana) result in the development of certain outcomes or 'fruits' (phala). Again it is simple cause and effect. If you sow an apple seed you can only reasonably expect to produce an apple tree. Obviously, moral choices aren't really seeds and we can't always predict the outcomes of certain choices. However, according to the Buddha, what we have to do is act for the right reasons or intentions and think through what are the most likely consequences of our actions. Putting both of these together means that we're far more likely to 'do the right thing' than not.

Roots and branches

Anything which grows depends on good roots. The state of the roots determines the quality of the plant. The Buddha taught that whether an action can be considered good or bad is a mixture of good intention and good consequences. The intentions of an action can have bad roots or good roots.

There are three forms of bad root (Akusala):

◆ choices based on greed

◆ choices based on delusion

◆ choices based on hatred.

It's obvious that if we make choices based on these things, then even if we are aiming for something 'good' or if something 'good' comes out of it, then calling that a 'good' choice is still questionable.

On the other hand, there are three forms of good root (Kusala):

◆ choices based on non-attachment

◆ choices based on understanding

◆ choices based on kindness.

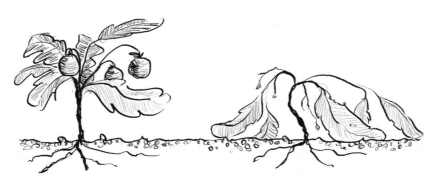

Choices based on the forms of good root can still result in bad outcomes – that's cause and effect for you. But the Buddha suggested that once you made your choices based on Kusala rather than Akusala, good is more likely to follow. Can this approach help Mr Bongle who is no doubt feeling a bit down because his kindness towards Bart resulted in Bart's life taking a turn for the worse? Probably. Mr Bongle should perhaps have shown a little more understanding of Bart's situation. Perhaps Mr Bongle should have been a more realistic about what Bart was likely to do with any money he got. If Mr Bongle had just given Bart a sandwich instead of money, then the negative consequences of Bart's using the money to buy wine could never have arisen (although they might have happened after a different donation of money at another time). There is no easy solution to this problem, but a little more understanding wouldn't have hurt. If the roots are right (good), then it's more likely that the branches will be too. Remember too that the consequences of actions can be for you or for others (and so again you, indirectly), and that these consequences determine the Kammic patterns you set up for the next rebirth. Your Kammic formations follow you throughout your rebirths and either tie you to or free you from the Samsaric cycle. So what you think or do now may not catch up with you for a few rebirths yet, but it will eventually.

The Dhamma as medicine

The Buddha's words were medicines for a given sickness at a given time – always infinitely adaptable to the conditions of the audience

Source: Van Hien as quoted at www.buddhanet.net

Skilful and unskilful actions

You could get yourself tied up in theoretical discussion about what makes something good or bad, but Buddhists are more interested in the practicalities, and how this question of what makes an action good or bad affects the way you live your life. For Buddhists, the notions of good and bad Kamma rest upon the idea of skilful and unskilful actions.

Before exploring the concept of skilful and unskilful actions, it is worth remembering one of the key features of Buddhism. There are many guidelines about how to live as a Buddhist, and different Buddhist groups follow different sets of 'rules' for living (more of that later), but the number one rule as taught by the Buddha himself was, as covered earlier, 'If you don't like it, you know what you can do with it' (see page 14). The Buddha did not teach a set of inflexible rules or laws, and there is no Buddhist God or gods to check if you are sticking to these laws anyway. (There is, of course, the Kammic law of cause and effect. But that is a different kind of 'law'.) Buddhists adopt a 'suck it and see' approach to life. Trying to live your life well demands that you are sensibly flexible when you need to be and that you treat 'rules' as guidelines which can be ignored if the need arises. So the concept of skilful and unskilful actions is all about approaching life's difficulties in a creative and insightful way.

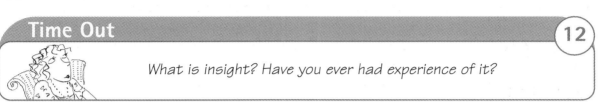

Time Out 12

What is insight? Have you ever had experience of it?

Talk Point 18

In your opinion, is there any action or choice which is always wrong (that is, regardless of the context)?

The idea of skilful and unskilful actions shows that the Buddhist must take many factors into account when making a moral choice, including the setting in which the choice is made; this means that different decisions, made in different circumstances, can lead to different outcomes. This could mean that completely different choices could both be right – even if they lead to different outcomes. Buddhist must take three things into account when assessing the skilfulness or unskilfulness of actions: the intentions, the foreseen consequences, and the appropriateness of the act to the person doing the act.

Actions are based on intentions

An action is wrong if the person doing it has based his decision on one of the three bad roots above. It is wrong if the intention was wrong. This means that if you do something good only to gain an advantage for yourself, then your action is wrong. An example would be inviting a loner to your birthday party only so you get another present, not because you want to be kind to that person. This would be an unskilful action.

It is not always easy to be definite about the intention behind an action, but the Buddha taught that if it is based on one of the three good roots then it is more likely to be well intentioned. An example of a skilful action might be a 'white lie'. Although telling the truth is usually the right thing to do, in some situations it would be very wrong. For example, imagine an angry person bursts into your class demanding to know where Kyle McHaggis is, and that it's obvious this

person probably wants to do something very nasty to Kyle. You know that Kyle is sitting right next to you and you notice that he has gone deathly white. The skilful action here would be to lie – tell the person that Kyle is not in school today – and give Kyle the chance to sort things out once the angry person has gone away and calmed down. The intention of your lie is good because you are doing something which you think is in Kyle's best interests, therefore it is a skilful action with good Kammic consequences.

Actions have consequences which can be foreseen

When a drunk driver causes an accident they almost always try to defend themselves by saying that they didn't *intend* to cause any harm. They probably didn't, but that's not the point. It's quite easy to foresee or know in advance that, if you drive a car while under the influence of alcohol, then you are more likely to make mistakes which could result in an accident. Any reasonable person can make that obvious link. So, when you decide on any course of action you've got to think it through to the best of your ability. Imagine that you believe that lying is always wrong, no matter what the circumstances, so you tell the angry person that Kyle is sitting beside you. It's obvious that your truth telling isn't likely to be helpful to Kyle at this moment. You can quite easily work out in advance that your action of truth telling might lead to dire consequences for Kyle. Similarly, if someone who has been drinking then drives a car and causes an accident, what they *intended* doesn't matter. Their action in driving the car was unskilful because they could have worked out that an accident was a likely effect of their action. The skilful action would have been to take a taxi home instead.

Actions are linked to the person who carries them out

What is right for one person to do might not be right for another. Your actions can be right or wrong depending upon the effect they are likely to have on you or according to your own situation. Here's an example. Many children in schools suffer from a condition called Attention Deficit Hyperactivity Disorder (ADHD). This makes their behaviour very unpredictable and can result in lots of problems for the sufferer as well as those around him or her. Recently it has been suggested that certain fizzy drinks make this condition worse for people who suffer it. So someone who doesn't have ADHD can drink fizzy stuff without any problem, but someone who has ADHD can't. Therefore an ADHD sufferer would be showing an unskilful action by drinking a fizzy drink. Of course, consequences are important here too, but it shows that what's perfectly acceptable for one person might not be for another. Similarly, killing an animal to eat when you're marooned on a

FIZZY DRINKS CAN MAKE ADHD WORSE!

desert island is a little different from killing to eat when you live next door to a supermarket. Different situations and types of person call for different choices; choosing the right course of action is the skilful thing.

Kammic consequences of actions

Skilful or unskilful actions therefore have Kammic consequences. Kamma builds up throughout this life and is carried over into the next rebirth. Add to this the Kammic consequences of your skilful or unskilful actions in previous rebirths and you've got a complicated mixture. Where you are right now and the life you currently lead is determined by the Kammic recipe you've been putting together for some time now. But don't be depressed or weighed down by this. Buddhists believe that the concept of Kammic consequences isn't about some kind of universal law crushing you into submission – it's really the opposite. Everything depends on you – your beliefs, your actions and your choices. You can make good or bad Kamma for yourself. You don't have to please a god or stick rigidly to unchangeable laws. You just have to make the right choices at the right time for the right reasons. If you do, you build up good Kamma. As you know already, this is very closely linked to your rebirths. It is also linked to your ultimate goal and that is the attainment of Enlightenment (Nibbana). The goal of living is to use this current life or rebirth to make progress towards Enlightenment. You are bound to the cycle of Samsara, but by using skilful actions you are trying to free yourself from being bound to this seemingly endless cycle of rebirth. To simplify, skilful actions will help you progress towards Enlightenment and escape from the cycle of Samsara. Unskilful actions, on the other hand, will just bind you even more closely to the cycle of Samsara and the state of being unenlightened or ignorant.

The Buddhist view of compassion

In the philosophy of Buddhism, compassion has two main aspects. First, as a desirable quality in human character, it is meant to regulate our attitude to other people. Secondly, it has its transcendental aspect known as great or grand compassion found only in sages like Buddhas, Boddhisattvas and Arhats. . . it 'seeketh not its own'. . . The best way [to relieve the suffering of others] is to lead them to the freedom of buddhahood.

Source: Encyclopaedia of Religions. Malasekera: Vol 4

May no one deceive another, nor despise him in anyway anywhere. Let no one wish another ill, owing to him anger or provocation.

Just as a mother would protect her son – her only son – with her life – even so let him cultivate this boundless love to all human beings.

Source: Karaniya Metta Sutta

Compassion leads to loving kindness

One way Buddhists try to make sure that their actions are always more likely to be skilful than unskilful is to exercise *compassion*. Basing your choices on the three good roots as opposed to the bad ones is more likely to happen where you demonstrate this key Buddhist ideal. All life involves suffering so you should react to this by trying to understand that everything is suffering. This awareness of suffering should lead you to act always and everywhere with compassion (Karuna). This is a central Buddhist idea which tries to sum up everything covered in this section. Compassion is about being aware of the fact that everything is experiencing suffering, and using this awareness to make sure that all your actions have the goal of getting rid of or reducing the effects of that suffering.

Being compassionate is a whole state of mind and an approach to everything you do. If you act in a spirit of compassion then you're never really likely to go wrong, no matter what you do. Being compassionate means that you'll take possible consequences into account, act in a way suited to the situation (or your own abilities), and act with the best of intentions. So being compassionate covers all the possibilities and is a simple but pretty effective philosophy for living. Compassion will always lead to positive actions and is far more likely to lead to exercising skilful actions.

Compassion will express itself in the form of loving kindness (Metta). Loving kindness is simply shorthand for compassion-in-action. It is like the 'tough love' which people talk about these days. It's not some kind of passive soppiness, but an active and skilful way of putting compassion into practical action which then leads to good Kammic consequences.

Talk Point (19)

What do you understand by 'tough love'?

Loving kindness isn't just a state of mind, it leads to real action. This is why Buddhists believe that their life should contribute positively to the world in which they live, and why they don't think that just retreating into a temple and meditating is the only way to attain Enlightenment. Some people think that Buddhism is a very inward-looking and essentially selfish faith. The idea of active loving kindness shows that this just isn't true. Buddhists around the world are involved in all kinds of activities which aim to promote social benefits and make people's lives easier. This can be a big or small action – whether helping someone dying from HIV/AIDS or making your mum a cup of tea – and it is all based on compassion.

Compassion

The rationale for universal compassion is based on the same principle of spiritual democracy. It is the recognition of the fact that every living being has an equal right to and desire for happiness. The true acceptance of [this] requires that we think and act in terms of the common good. Compassion and universal responsibility require a commitment to personal sacrifice and the neglect of egotistical desires.

Source: The Dalai Lama, as quoted at www.dharmakara.net

Loving kindness in action

Monks in Thailand and South-East Asia have always helped the community in various ways. As the spread of HIV/AIDS has made its way through South-East Asia, monks decided they should find out about this and help those affected by it. They realised that the duty of a monk has three parts:

1 To learn through study and meditation

2 To wander and teach for people's well-being

3 To be a place of refuge for those suffering.

The monks believed that the HIV/AIDS problem was rooted in ignorance and their job was to uproot that ignorance. The Sangha Metta project was set up in Chiang Mai, Thailand. Monks are trained in HIV/AIDS prevention and care. They educate people about the threat of HIV/AIDS and then care for those who suffer from it, as well as helping the children of sufferers. Children made orphans by HIV/AIDS are taken in by temples. This practical approach has spread across South-East Asia: Ky Quang II Pagoda in Ho Chi Min City, Vietnam, supports almost 200 orphaned children.

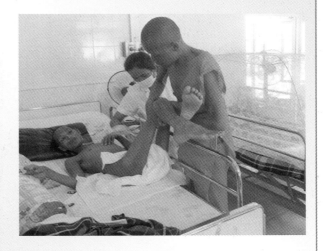

Source: based on information at www.buddhanet.net

Compassion, loving kindness and Nibbana

In very difficult circumstances, these Thai monks are performing skilful actions based on compassion, leading to practical action of loving kindness. Before the monks began this programme of practical education, some members of the

community would not even walk past the house of someone with HIV/AIDS because they were afraid of catching it. The monks' example changed this view and helped people address their ignorance of this issue. This is a very clear example of how compassion leads towards Enlightenment – the removal of ignorance. For Buddhists, of course, it's more than that – it's a step on the road to Nibbana.

Activities

Knowledge, Understanding, Evaluation

1 Do you think Bhikku Amforashandi would have wanted to win his round on 'Mastermind'? Should he have wanted to win?

2 What does the Second Noble Truth state?

3 Should a Buddhist have goals of any kind? Explain your answer.

4 In what way might a goal in life be just another example of cause and effect?

5 In what ways is Kamma like kicking a football?

6 Why might some Buddhists believe that everything that happens to you is the result of Kamma?

7 In what way do other Buddhists disagree with this?

8 Explain how Kamma can be an action as well as a result.

9 In what way is Kamma like a seed?

10 What did Mr Bongle and Mr Bungle do? Which of them did the right thing? Explain your answer fully.

11 What, in your opinion, makes an action right or wrong? Explain.

12 What did the Buddha suggest you had to do to make sure that you were more likely to be doing the right thing?

13 In your own words, describe the three good roots.

14 How can making the wrong choice affect you as well as others? Give an example to explain your thinking.

15 In what way can the Buddha's teaching be thought of as medicine?

16 Explain the three things Buddhists have to take into account in order to practise skilful actions.

17 How do unskilful actions bind you to the cycle of Samsara?

18 Give an example from your own experience of acting with good intention.

19 Describe a time when you had to think very carefully about the possible consequences of a choice you had to make (or perhaps a time when you didn't think carefully enough).

20 What does it mean to say that an action might be right for one person and not for another? Give an example from your own experience.

21 How is Kamma related to skilful and unskilful actions?

22 Why would a Buddhist not be miserable about the consequences of Kamma?

23 How does exercising skilful actions lead to good Kamma?

24 Why is good Kamma desirable?

25 How can a Buddhist be sure that his actions are more likely to be skilful than unskilful?

26 How does compassion help to avoid the Three Root Poisons?

27 What is 'loving kindness'?

28 What does the Dalai Lama say is the rationale (reason for) compassion?

29 In what ways are the activities of the Thai monks working on the Sangha Metta project examples of loving kindness?

30 In your area, who or what needs loving kindness?

THE GOALS

Practical Activities

1 Write a letter which might be sent by a Buddhist who had been watching the 'Mastermind' show on which Bhikku Amforashandi appeared. What might the Buddhist say about how the Bhikku was treated?

2 Draw an image which demonstrates the idea that the 'seed' of Kamma grows and leads to 'fruits'.

3 Debate in class: 'Mr Bongle and Mr Bungle both did the right thing'.

4 Design a collage or other piece of artwork which illustrates the three bad and three good roots.

5 Make up a series of moral dilemmas. Create a number of characters who have to respond to these imaginary dilemmas. For each character, work out what you think would be the skilful action in relation to each dilemma.

6 In groups work out how you could be a more compassionate person. How could your school act in a more compassionate way? Design a questionnaire about this and display your findings.

Unit Assessment Question

Int 1 Why should a Buddhist show compassion to all living things? *(4)*

Int 2 How does Kamma help you towards Enlightenment? *(6)*

Higher

'For hate is not conquered by hate: hate is conquered by love.' (Dhammapada) Why is compassion important for Buddhists? *(8)*

THE GOALS

Sample Exam Question

Int 1 Give one example of what a Buddhist would call a skilful action. *(2KU)*

Int 2 'Kamma is central to Buddhism.' Would a Buddhist agree? Give reasons for your answer. *(2KU, 4AE)*

Higher

'Unskilful actions bind the unenlightened to Samsara.' What would a Buddhist mean by this? *(8KU)*

Homework

Cut out a newspaper article which you think demonstrates loving kindness in action (it doesn't have to be linked to Buddhism). Be prepared to explain in class why this is an example of loving kindness.

Personal Reflection

Try out this skilful actions challenge. During the course of a week note down any moral choices you have to make. For each one, think about what the skilful action would be according to what you have learned so far about Buddhism. (You can keep all of this to yourself – you don't have to share it with anyone unless you want to.) At the end of the week reflect on your own answer to this question: how much compassion do you show to living things?

Nibbana

A game for all the family! Play ... Nibbana!

Catch that Third Noble Truth© as its meaning tries to evade you! Go from ignorance to bliss! Wake up to the true nature of Reality! And finally ... become one with Reality! Stand before those chilling fires that lead to rebirth. Build up your Kamma through countless lives and give yourself the power to ... blow those fires out!

This great game for all the family comes with different Buddha characters (Chubby Buddha, Skinny Buddha and of course, Middle Way Buddha) to mark your progress towards Enlightenment. There are two routes you can choose to follow – the Theravada™ route and the Mahayana™ route.

Game 1
If you take the Theravada™ route then you'll have to become an Arhat. This will take loads of suffering-filled lifetimes. Throughout each lifetime you'll have to stick to that Noble Eightfold Path – but watch out – you can go down as well as up! Start as a stream entrant – but remember the stream only flows one way and, as every Buddhist knows, you can never step in the same stream twice! Try those cheats to make your game easier if you can't stand the pace ... simply become a nun or monk and watch the lives whizz by! But be careful – if you're too individualistic then you'll have problems. And whatever you do ... don't become a selfish Arhat or by contradicting yourself you'll just cancel yourself out and you'll have to start all over again!!!

Game 2

The Mahayana™ route's different, but just as tricky a way to play altogether. Here, the game plan is to become a Bodhisattva. With this, even once you've gained Enlightenment, you carry on playing by working for the Enlightenment of others! You get the benefits of their benefits ... and even if you don't you still win! (But be careful you don't desire that – you'll lose loads of points that way!) You might have to put off your own entry to Nibbana once or twice – but don't worry – it's all part of the game. In this version you could even aim to become Avalokiteshvara and grow a thousand arms to help a thousand people – imagine!

The game is over when you attain Nibbana. How will you know you've won? Wait and see – you'll have to experience it first!!!

Nibbana

Tarquin was in sixth year. You know the type – he has loads of Higher As in things like nuclear physics and astronomy. He decided to do RMPS for a small break, thinking it wouldn't tax someone of his brilliance too much. He's going to his RMPS teacher to pick up his prelim marks. He thought he was particularly smart in his answers, especially the one about Nibbana. 'Explain what Buddhists understand by Nibbana' was the question and Tarquin's answer was a stroke of genius – or so he thought. He left the page blank – that was his answer. On receiving his marked prelim paper Tarquin noticed with some puzzlement that he'd failed. His star answer to the Nibbana question hadn't been marked – in fact there was no mark there at all. When he asked his RMPS teacher why this was so, the RMPS teacher responded like this: 'Tarquin, this question asked you to show that you understood the idea of Nibbana. If you truly understood Nibbana, then you would also understand the mark I gave you.' Tarquin was well and truly outsmarted this time... so much for nuclear physics and astronomy!

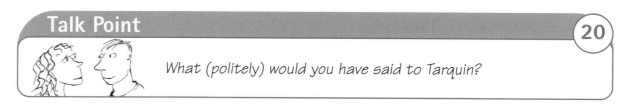

Talk Point

(20)

What (politely) would you have said to Tarquin?

What is Nibbana?

So is Nibbana something, or is it nothing at all as Tarquin seems to be suggesting? The Sanskrit word for Nibbana is Nirvana. This comes from two words: *Nir* which means out and *va* which means to blow. So it is often thought that Nibbana is something which is blown out. But what remains after you've blown something out? By definition, nothing. So was Tarquin right after all? Would a blank page properly explain Nibbana? Sadly for Tarquin and his reputation as a genius, no. Remember that, for Buddhists, the flames of suffering are fuelled by greed, hatred and ignorance.

When the individual has withdrawn the power for these flames, the flames go out – and that is when Nibbana is attained. But don't think of Nibbana as being like a candle which has gone out. It is where the fuel that provided greed, hatred and ignorance is no longer present (so the candle isn't lit in the first place).

Nibbana is not heaven. The Buddha wasn't concerned by the issue of whether a person exists in some form after death or 'where they go'. He refused even to answer the question about whether someone who was enlightened existed after death because 'after death' isn't the point – the here and now is.

The problem about Nibbana is that it is easier to explain what it is not rather than what it is. Maybe poor Tarquin was on to something after all, but he might have got some marks if he had tried to explain his position. His blank page suggested that words weren't enough to explain Nibbana, and in that respect he was right. According to the Buddha, Nibbana cannot be *explained* – it can only be *experienced*. However, some explanation is needed to help you have some understanding of what it is all about.

> ### Time Out (13)
>
>
>
> *Can you think of anything else which can't be described in words and can only be experienced?*

Waking up to the way things are

The Third Noble Truth states: Once you have ceased craving you will cease suffering and you will attain Nibbana. Nibbana is a state of mind (or existence) which can also be understood as Enlightenment or liberation. It can be achieved or attained while you are still alive. It is a state where personal existence, entity, death, rebirth and consciousness, and so on no longer have any meaning. It is where you have succeeded in removing from your life (or liberating yourself from) the fuel which is hatred, greed and delusion. These are the things which fuel Samsara and lead to rebirth. Without them, the force driving the cycle of Samsara is removed, and the endless cycle stops (as if the power is switched off), and there is no more rebirth.

You can have Nibbana now, but you won't know what it means until you have it. (So this book can't tell you what it means, either.) It's not the kind of thing you tell everyone about. If you feel the need to show off that you have attained Nibbana, then you're living in ignorance and you haven't actually attained Nibbana at all. In the film *Babe*, the sheep pig eventually wakes up to 'the way things are'. Previously he had been deluded into thinking that the truck which took animals to the slaughterhouse was taking them to some kind of desirable paradise. When he became aware of what was really happening he took the first step to Enlightenment. But then he worked hard to preserve his own life, or rather the illusion of his own existence. And this attachment to his own life demonstrated that he hadn't achieved full Enlightenment yet.

So Nibbana is about two important things: (i) waking up to Reality, and (ii) becoming one with Reality (that is, acting consistently with this awareness of Reality).

Talk Point

Is Nibbana something or not something?

Understanding Nibbana

Nibbana is not existence, hardly can it be non-existence. It lies totally beyond both existence and non-existence. [. . .] Nibbana which is incomprehensible and profound can only be realised by those who have attained it and thus passed beyond both limitations, existence and non-existence.

Source: www.triplegem.org.u

Theravada and Mahayana sects

Earlier in the Introduction, this book briefly described the history of Buddhism after the Buddha and how two sects – the Theravada sect and the Mahayana sect – developed. The Theravada sect and the Mahayana sect have slightly different views on the 'best' way to go about attaining Nibbana.

Theravada sect and Arhats

Theravadin view of Nibbana

Nibbana is a state attained by the complete liberation from *dukkha*. . . A person who has attained the state of *Nibbana* will no longer acquire *kamma* that keeps the cycle of life going, hence there will no longer be rebirth. [. . .] *Nibbana* is to be attained in this life, not after death. [. . .] An enlightened person will have developed an intuitive wisdom (*sati panna*) which enables him to see the true nature of the world, i.e. [. . .] *dukkha*, *anicca* and *anatta*.

Source: www.londonbuddhistvihara.co.uk/qa/qa_nibbana.htm

The Theravada Buddhist sect believes that there are three areas of personal development which you have to work on to reach Nibbana. These areas are:

- Sila (morality)
- Samadhi (concentration)
- Panna (wisdom).

All of these have to be, in the words of Baby Bear, 'just right' to enable you to progress towards Enlightenment. One without the other is not enough. (Later in this book, these are also described as the Threefold Way.)

Theravada Buddhists also believe that to attain Nibbana you must become an Arhat. This involves four stages of progression:

1 Sotapanna – this is known as the 'stream entrant'. A person enters this stage when they have lost the three fetters of self-illusion (Sakkaya-ditthi), doubts (Vicikiccha) and clinging to vain rituals and rites (Silabbata paramasa). (A fetter is something which ties you to things, holding you back, and preventing you from moving on.) In the same way that a stream flows only one way – towards its final destination – so the stream-entrant is flowing towards Enlightenment.

2 Sakadagami – this person is a 'once returner'. By now this person has weakened the hold which sensual craving (Kamaraga) and ill-will (Patigha) have on people. This person has only one more major rebirth ahead of them before they attain Nibbana.

3 Anagami – this person has now managed to completely eliminate sensual craving and ill-will from their life. This person won't be reborn in this world or in any of the realms of sense-pleasure (think back to the realms depicted in the wheel of life).

4 Arhat – becoming an Arhat is the 'top prize' for the Theravada Buddhist, because this means they have attained Nibbana. This person has destroyed the five remaining fetters which are: pride/conceit (Mana); restlessness (Uddhacca); ignorance (Avijja); craving for existence in the world of form (Rupa-raga) and craving for existence in the non-material world (Arupa-raga).

THE GOALS

So, in order to become an Arhat, the person has fully extinguished all defilements, as well as progressed through all the types of existence and as such is the 'perfected saint' of Buddhism. Theravada Buddhists believe that becoming an Arhat takes many lifetimes and it involves adhering rigorously to the Noble Eightfold Path of Buddhism. You are more likely to become an Arhat if you are a monk or nun than if you are an ordinary person or a lay person. This is because the daily responsibilities and obligations of an ordinary person (for example, job, family concerns, financial pressures) may interfere with trying to live according to the Noble Eightfold Path.

Can an Arhat become a Buddha (since the word 'Buddha' means 'Enlightened One')? No. By definition, a Buddha is a being which attains Nibbana by its own efforts, and since an Arhat attains Nibbana by following the teachings of others – most obviously Buddhas – then they cannot become a Buddha.

Finally, some non-Theravada Buddhists (and some non-Buddhists for that matter) believe that becoming an Arhat is really quite a selfish thing, because it requires you to spend a lot of time and energy on . . . yourself, and such self-absorption seems contrary to the spirit of Buddhism. However, Theravada Buddhists respond to such criticism by saying that the Buddha taught that when you have attained Nibbana the first thing you should do is teach others so they can attain it too, and that this is what they do.

Time Out 14

Do you think you could spot an Arhat?

Mahahana sect and Bodhisattvas

The Mahayana tradition believes that the route of the Arhat is too remote from what most ordinary people would be able to achieve, given the interference of daily life. They argue that everyone should be able to attain Nibbana, not just those few who are able to follow everything to the letter by living a monastic life. The Mahayana tradition sees itself as the 'big ox-cart' because it can accommodate so many more people than the Theravada (the 'lesser vehicle').

The whole idea of the Bodhisattva (or 'becoming-Buddha') began as a way to explain the previous lives of the Buddha. What was he doing before the life when, as Siddartha Gautama, he finally found his way to Nibbana? Mahayana Buddhists believe that what he was doing was being a Bodhisattva, a Buddha-to-be or a becoming-Buddha. In a manner of speaking he was perfecting his craft, heading towards his eventual Buddhahood. His previous rebirths are told in the funny and sometimes weird Jataka Tales.

THE GOALS

A Jataka Tale: *A Gang of Drunkards*

Once upon a time, when Brahmadatta was king, the Enlightenment Being was born in a wealthy family. He became the richest man in Benares.

There also happened to be a gang of drunkards who roamed the streets. All they ever thought about was finding ways to get alcohol, the drug they thought they couldn't live without.

One day, when they had run out of money as usual, they came up with a scheme to rob the richest man in Benares. But they didn't realise that he was the reborn Bodhisattva, so he wouldn't be so easy to fool!

They decided to make a 'Mickey Finn', which is a drink of liquor with a sleeping drug secretly added to it. Their plan was to get the rich man to drink the Mickey Finn. Then when he fell asleep they would rob all his money, jewellery, and even the rich clothes he wore. So they set up a temporary little roadside bar. They put their last remaining liquor into a bottle, and mixed in some strong sleeping pills.

Later the rich man came by on his way to the palace. One of the alcoholics called out to him, 'Honourable sir, why not start your day right – by having a drink with us? And the first one is on the house!' Then he poured a glass of the dishonest liquor. But the Enlightenment Being did not drink any form of alcohol. Nevertheless, he wondered why these drunkards were being so generous with their favourite drug. It just wasn't like them.

He realised it must be some kind of trick. So he decided to teach them a lesson. He said, 'It would be an insult to appear before the king in a drunken state, or with even the slightest smell of liquor on my breath. But please be so kind as to wait for me here. I'll see you again when I return from the palace.' The drunkards were disappointed. They would not be able to drink again as soon as they wanted. But they decided to be patient and wait.

Later that day the rich man came back to the little roadside bar. The alcoholics were getting desperate for a drink. They called him over and said, 'Honourable sir, why not celebrate your visit to the king? Have a drink of this fine liquor. Remember, the first one is free!'

But the rich man just kept looking at the liquor bottle and glass. He said, 'I don't trust you. That bottle and glass of liquor are exactly as they were this morning. If it were as good as you say it is, you would have tasted some yourselves by now. In fact, you couldn't help but drink it all! I'm no fool. You must have added another drug to the alcohol.' The richest man in Benares went on his way, and the gang of drunkards went back to their plotting and scheming.

Source: www.buddhanet.net/bt_3.htm

Talk Point

What's the message here?

22

The word Bodhisattva means 'Enlightened Being' or 'Enlightened Essence'. (An essence is something which is central to the existence of something else, giving it an overall 'flavour'.) Mahayana Buddhists think that being an Arhat is admirable, but it misses the very thing that the Buddha wanted for everyone, and that is wellbeing for everyone and the chance for everyone to attain Nibbana. The Bodhisattva is to be respected, because he could just turn his back on everyone else and blow out his own flames of rebirth, enter Nibbana and pull the door closed behind him. But the Bodhisattva doesn't do this. He deliberately chooses to stay in the Samsaric cycle in order to help the unenlightened reach Nibbana. Some Bodhisattvas (who, by definition, have 'qualified' for Nibbana) vow not to enter it until they have helped a certain number of people reach it too.

Even though Buddhism has no God or gods, to many in the Mahayana tradition, Bodhisattvas like Avalokiteshvara (the Dalai Lama) have become so spiritually developed that they have become – in effect – gods (or at least godly). In Mahayana Buddhism too, people might pray to gods or bow to them and worship them (though not in the same way as theistic religions), because they think Bodhisattvas will then help them. Critics complain that this isn't what the Buddha taught at all. Mahayana Buddhists reply that the Buddha did tell us to try things out for ourselves and see how they worked, so there's nothing wrong with some demi-god worship if it seems to work.

Instructions for becoming a Bodhisattva

1   Develop Bodhicitta – this is the mind of Enlightenment. This is where you consciously decide that you want to become a bodhisattva. You can train this mind in six areas which are known as the six perfections:

2   Develop generosity (Dana) – this means to give with no thought for yourself.

3   Develop morality (Sila) – this means being mindful of consequences will help you make the right moral choices. A good moral choice is one which refrains from causing any harm to yourself or those around you.

4   Develop patience (Ksanti) – because being patient will help you put up with life's problems.

5   Develop effort or perseverance (Virya) – unless you work at it (and it won't be easy) you can't become a Bodhisattva.

6 Develop concentration (Dhyana) – this means keeping your mind focused and your thoughts clear.

7 Develop wisdom (Prajna) – once you've developed the previous five perfections, you will also have developed wisdom. You will also understand Anicca and Anatta (see pages 41–43).

As you follow these instructions you are likely to go through other stages on your way to Bodhisattvahood:

◆ Sravaka – anyone looking for liberation/Enlightenment

◆ Pratyekabuddha – someone who has attained Nibbana but who can't reveal the truth to others, such as a Samyakssambuddha

◆ Bodhisattva – one who has attained Nibbana and is able to tell others about it and help them to achieve it too.

The Bodhisattva is the perfect combination of the two key principles of Buddhism – wisdom (Prajna) and compassion (Karuna). Having perfected these means that the Bodhisattva has also perfected the performing of skilful actions. A Bodhisattva will always know what the right thing to do will be in any situation to help someone along the road to Nibbana.

The Bodhisattva view

Compassion – empathy with the suffering of the world and a desire to rescue all living things from it – is vital to the decision to keep on postponing the entrance to the bliss of nibbana and to continue being reborn; and wisdom is essential to a deeper and deeper understanding, through successive lives, of the emptiness (sanyata) of all there is.

Source: The Essence of Buddhism, by Jo Durden Smith

To sum up: you can attain Nibbana and still live on normally in this world. The Buddha did. In fact he lived to the ripe old age of 80 – a fully Enlightened Being. Once you have attained Nibbana you still have to eat and sleep, and you can still experience the normal range of human emotions, but because you are Enlightened these emotions won't hold on to you the way they used to. You will have wakened up to the way things are and you will no longer be ignorant about Reality.

Time Out

Do you think that you are 'asleep'?

THE GOALS

Activities

Knowledge, Understanding, Evaluation

1 Why did Tarquin fail his RMPS prelim?

2 Do you think his teacher was right to fail him?

3 How do the Three Root Poisons fuel rebirth?

4 What happens when fuel is taken away from a fire?

5 What did the Buddha say about what happens to you after death?

6 'Nibbana can not be explained, it can only be experienced.' What does this mean? Do you agree?

7 Could a blank page explain Nibbana? Explain your answer.

8 Does someone have to die before they experience Nibbana?

9 How does Nibbana 'switch off' Samsara?

10 Had the sheep pig in *Babe* become enlightened?

11 According to the triplegem source, who can understand (realise) Nibbana?

12 According to Theravada Buddhists, what are the three areas of personal development you have to go through on the road to Nibbana?

13 What do Theravada Buddhists think you have to become before you attain Enlightenment?

14 How do you become a 'stream entrant'?

15 What has a 'once returner' managed to do?

16 What will an Anagami not have to do?

17 What has an Arhat managed to achieve?

18 Why is becoming an Arhat difficult? What might you have to do to help yourself become one?

19 Why is an Arhat not a Buddha?

20 What should an Arhat do as soon as he becomes an Arhat?

21 What was the Buddha in his previous rebirths?

22 What could a Bodhisattva do and why doesn't he do it?

23 Why might a Mahayana Buddhist bow to a Bodhisattva?

24 In your own words, describe the seven steps to becoming a Bodhisattva.

25 What two things does the Bodhisattva 'perfectly combine'?

26 How does Nibbana remove ignorance?

Practical Activities

1 Think about the computer game idea at the start of this section. Now think about the Bodhisattva and the Arhat.

Make up character cards for them, imagining that they are participants in the game. What qualities will each have?

2 Design an information leaflet for younger pupils (for example, S1) which explains the Buddhist idea of Nibbana.

3 Create images of Sila, Samadhi and Panna.

4 Make up a snakes and ladders game based on the four stages of becoming an Arhat and the seven instructions for becoming a Bodhisattva.

5 Act out the Jataka tale or make a storyboard based on it. Make sure you explain what the message in the story is.

6 Imagine a Bodhisattva and an Arhat meet. What would their conversation be like?

Unit Assessment Question

Int 1 What is Nibbana? *(2)*

Int 2 'If you have not attained Nibbana you remain in ignorance.' What would a Buddhist mean by this statement? *(6)*

Higher

'Nibbana means awakening to the true nature of reality.' Explain this Buddhist teaching. *(8)*

Sample Exam Question

Int 1 Describe the Third Noble Truth. *(2KU)*

Int 2 According to Mahayana Buddhists, what is a Bodhisattva? *(4 KU)*

Higher

What criticisms of the idea of the Bodhisattva might a Theravada Buddhist have? *(4KU)*

Homework

Design a 'Wanted' poster for either a Bodhisattva or an Arhat. Explain how you could identify them.

Personal Reflection

What are your views on Nibbana? Is it a state you want to achieve?

Enlightenment: Images of the Buddha

Many people's homes these days have a Buddha statue in them. People like the look of them even if they don't use them for any religious purpose. There are many different kinds of Buddha – some reflecting his earthly life, others showing aspects of his character, and others packed with Buddhist symbolism explaining bits of Buddhist belief.

Within Buddhism itself, images of the Buddha are used to help people understand parts of the faith, and the history of Buddhism. They are used to help people concentrate during meditation. They are even worshipped. Sometimes they are used as good luck charms. Some Buddhists believe that the images themselves can convey good Kamma. The number and styles of Buddha images is staggering and is often closely linked to the country where they originated. Buddha images therefore sometimes show features which are related to the religions which existed in the country before Buddhism arrived. Where Buddha images are found also varies. Some are little statues for your home. Some are vast ornate statues in temples. Others are carved out of solid rock in wild places. All have the same role – to remind people of the Buddha and his teaching and give a focus to the beliefs and practices of the faith.

Talk Point 23

Do you have any Buddha statues at home? Have you seen any recently anywhere else (apart maybe from RMPS)?

The Historical Buddha

Siddartha Gautama, who was to become the Buddha, lived and died on earth. He was a royal prince who became a holy man, the Enlightened One. He died, some say of accidental food poisoning, at the age of 80. Images of the Buddha show elements of his historical life.

The Buddha began life as a royal prince, with his every whim pampered and catered for. The film *Little Buddha* is a fairly accurate historical image of the young Siddartha.

After his visit to the village where he saw the four sights, he became a wandering holy man. During this time he joined a group of ascetics who starved themselves and treated themselves badly in the hope that this would help them to find happiness and spiritual fulfilment. Images of Siddartha at this time show him as a skeletal figure, punishing himself to try to achieve understanding.

Eventually he decided that self-punishment was not the way to find understanding and he vowed to sit under the bodhi tree until he attained Enlightenment. At this point, Mara the devil tried to tempt and distract him from his goal.

This image shows Siddartha to be serene in his response to Mara. There is no panic or fear shown – he is in control, accepting that Mara is trying to put him off but is unaffected by it. At the end of all this temptation, he finally attains Enlightenment or Nibbana. At this point, the images of the Buddha show him with his hand pointing down or touching his hand to the ground. It's interesting that these days people talk about being 'grounded' not just when their parents are punishing them but when they feel that they have 'got in touch' with something real – in touch with Reality itself, perhaps. The moment of the Buddha's Enlightenment is when he comes to realise the true nature of all things and to understand Reality. He also becomes one with it. Some Buddhists refer to this as the moment when he calls the Earth to witness his Enlightenment.

The Buddha is also shown at this moment of Enlightenment as having a halo around his head. This is just another indication that something very special was happening to him at this moment of his becoming the Buddha. This halo might be thought of as representing the energy which was present during this momentous event.

Time Out ⑯

Halos are common to several religions. Find out which other religions have them and what they stand for. What are the similarities and differences?

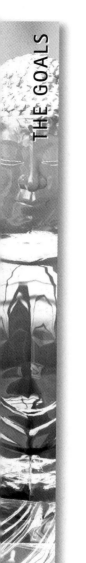

Following his Enlightenment, the Buddha gathered a group of disciples as his followers. Images show him teaching them the Dhamma or way towards their own Enlightenment.

This image reminds Buddhists that, even though he was Enlightened, the Buddha continued to live and die in the usual way, but that throughout his lifetime he tried to ensure that he passed on the way to Enlightenment to others.

At the end of his life, the Buddha died peacefully, reminding his disciples that death was just part of the natural cycle of life and not to be sad.

Death of the Buddha

Though he was very weak and weary, the Buddha was still addressing those present with words of exhortation. After addressing them the whole night the Blessed One spoke His last words, when it was nearing dawn, as follows: 'Behold, O disciples, I exhort you. Subject to decay are all conditioned things. Strive on with heedfulness'. The Buddha then attained the Ecstasies and arrived at the cessation of perception and sensation, and finally the Blessed One passed away; and there was an earthquake to mark His death.

Source: www.buddhistdoor.com

This is also called the Parinibbana of the Buddha – where his physical body ceases to exist and he attains his final Nibbana. In the Theravada tradition this is also what happens to the Arhat.

Sometimes the stage before the death of the Buddha is shown, where he is reclining awaiting his physical death and giving his final teachings to his disciples.

Talk Point

(24)

Some statues of Buddha are carved out of stone, as tall as buildings. Do you think making such things is a good thing for people to do?

Symbolism in Buddha images

So far these are all fairly straightforward images of the Buddha during his earthly life. You might have noticed, however, that sometimes Buddha images don't look much like a human being and sometimes they are covered with mysterious shapes and symbols. This is because the image of the Buddha is not just to remind you of his life on Earth but to remind you about his teachings, what he stood for and so on. A symbol is something which stands for or represents something else. Sometimes, images are posed in a certain way to remind us of times in the Buddha's life when he taught particular things. Images of the Buddha are usually shown standing, walking, sitting or reclining.

To simplify all of this, let's move from top to toe of the Buddha's image

Head

The top of the head reaches a point, which is called the Ushnisa. This might symbolise wisdom or it might just show the hairstyles of Indian men in the Buddha's day! There is a story that snails fell on to his head as he meditated under the bodhi tree. They stayed there to protect Buddha and died, where they remained.

In the centre of the forehead there is often a mark. Some Buddhists believe this is just a focal point to the image, helping with concentration, whereas others think it is symbolic of the Chakra or site of energy. Other Buddhists suggest that it represents the third way – a different way of seeing things which is not the same as the two physical eyes. This interpretation is be supported by the fact that the Buddha's eyes are most often shown closed. This is usually taken to mean that he is reflecting inwardly, perhaps symbolising the belief that we'll find Nibbana within ourselves rather than outside somewhere.

The ears of the Buddha are long. Again this could be a symbol for wisdom or it could be a mark of his royal background – as a wealthy prince his ear lobes would have been stretched by the wearing of heavy ornate jewellery. Whatever the individual features of the Buddha's head, the face is always shown to be calm, peaceful and contented.

Time Out 17

From what you know about Buddhism so far, why is the Buddha always shown as calm?

Neck

Images of the Buddha's neck often show lines which some claim are symbolic of the Buddha's rich and commanding voice. Some say that the shape of his neck looks like a vase, symbolising that he helped the sick. (In the Buddha's day, vases were the containers for medicines.)

Robes

The Buddha is almost always shown wearing the simple robes of a monk. His royal clothes are gone and he lives a simple life.

Hands

The hands of the Buddha are always long and elegant. In many images, his hands take up particular positions representing particular things. For example, his hands might be on his lap. This shows that he's meditating. The standing Buddha often has his hand raised. It might look as if he's telling you to stop, but he's not. This position represents fearlessness.

The Buddha's hands often take up particular shapes. These are called Mudras and each one has a different meaning.

For example, one hand resting over the other with both palms up is known as Dhyana, and it represents concentration. Another example, known as Vitarka, shows the thumb touching the forefinger, and is thought to represent teaching. Some say that this pose simply shows the Buddha running through the Four Noble Truths and using each finger to identify each one.

Dhyana hand shape

Vitarka hand shape

Feet

There was a time when it was forbidden to show images of the Buddha, so his footprints were depicted instead, and these were often highly decorated with symbols. In images of the Buddha, his feet are bare, but they are also often marked with symbols. These symbols have many various meanings.

The Buddha's feet

The soles of the Buddha's feet are said to be flat with all the toes of equal length. On each sole there are one hundred and eight auspicious marks (mangala lakkhana), with

the wheel (chakra) the principal mark at the centre while around it are grouped figures of animals, inhabitants of various worlds and other kinds of symbols. The idea is that all things are subject to the Buddha who is lord of all, and under whose feet are all things.

Source: www.ebudhaindia.com/srilanka/sripada.htm

Other objects associated with Buddha images

The Buddha is often shown holding an object in his hands. These objects have symbolic meanings. He may be holding a bowl, signifying his simple life where he had to depend on the generosity of others for his survival (a far cry from his royal upbringing).

This image also shows the Buddha in the traditional position of sitting on a lotus flower. The lotus flower is a symbol of purity and it reminds Buddhists that, just as the lotus flower grows from the murky depths of a pond to rise to the surface as a beautiful flower, so too the unenlightened can move from ignorance to Nibbana.

THE GOALS

The symbolism of the lotus flower

Starting life as a seed, it grows in the muddy darkness at the bottom of a pond. The darkness is like our ignorance – we can't clearly see the truth about life. The seed grows toward the warmth and light of the sun just as humans naturally grow toward the warmth of love and compassion, and toward the light of truth. The mature flower floats on the surface, bathing in the full light of the sun, well 'anchored' but moving freely according to the flow of the water – the changing current of any situation.

Source: www.buddhamind.info/leftside/arty/lotus.htm

As well as images of the historical Buddha, Buddhism has many images which have become part of the faith. These show clear links to the places where they are found and used in different ways. They are not the same as the historical Buddha, even though they sometimes show aspects of Buddhist teaching which he might have been comfortable with – but not always! For example, there is the 'laughing Buddha' who was a Chinese monk called Ho Tai. The Chinese people believed he was a reincarnation of the Buddha. He is thought to be a figure of good luck – people believe that if you rub his belly you'll be lucky, just as he obviously was (as shown by his happy face and well fed stomach).

Talk Point   25

What do you think of good and bad luck? Can you get it by rubbing a statue's belly?

In Tibet, huge paintings known as Thangkas depict images of Buddha. These are very colourful and elaborate; they used to help with meditation, as well as being objects of worship in their own right. The Thangka opposite is of the medicine Buddha, popular in Mahayana Buddhism.

The medicine Buddha

Medicine Buddha is one of many buddhas who have attained the state of perfect enlightenment for the benefit of all sentient beings. The enlightened mind has eliminated all negativity and perfected all positive qualities.

Medicine Buddha's blue sky-colored holy body signifies omniscient wisdom and compassion as vast as limitless space and is particularly associated with healing both mental and physical suffering.

Source: www.medicinebuddha.org

Whatever the form or symbolism of an individual image of the Buddha, they all represent the same general theme. The Buddha was a being who lived a historical life on Earth and who then attained Enlightenment. After this he lived on until his physical death. Images of him help to recall his life and help to focus people's lives on what he did and taught. Symbols also help people to understand Buddhist ideas. Understanding all of this helps the individual progress towards the ultimate goal of life – Nibbana.

Activities

Knowledge, Understanding, Evaluation

1 Why might someone who is not a Buddhist have a Buddha image in their home?

2 What are images of the Buddha used for?

3 In what kinds of places can you find Buddha images?

4 What is the very thin Buddha meant to show?

5 How is the Buddha shown when Mara was trying to tempt him?

6 What does the Buddha do with his hand at the moment of Enlightenment? Why?

7 What might a halo around the Buddha's head represent?

8 How is the Buddha shown at the point of his Parinibbana?

9 What is a symbol?

10 Describe the Buddha's hairstyle. What does it symbolise?

11 Why does the Buddha have long ears?

12 What does the mark in the centre of the Buddha's forehead stand for?

13 Why are the Buddha's eyes closed?

14 How is the Buddha usually dressed? Why?

15 Explain the meaning of one Mudra.

16 Why are the soles of Buddha's feet often covered with symbols?

17 What does the Buddha often sit on? What does this mean?

18 Who is Ho Tai and what are you supposed to do to him?

19 How is a Thangka used?

20 How do images of the Buddha help Buddhists?

Practical Activities

1 Make your own Buddha using any material you like. Try to stick to the 'rules' for making Buddhas. You can find these on the Internet. Be respectful as you make it and think of where and how it will be displayed.

2 Make a class display of images of the Buddha. For each one, write underneath an explanation of the image.

Unit Assessment Question

Int 1 Describe how one image of the Buddha you have studied illustrates the idea of Enlightenment. *(4)*

Sample Exam Question

Int 1 Explain why this image shows the Buddha looking like this. *(4KU)*

Homework

Find one piece of information about Buddha images which you have not already learned in this book.

Personal Reflection

What do you use to help you focus and concentrate?

THE GOALS

Textual Sources

Dhammapada 1–14

Dhammapada text	Commentary
1 What we are today comes from our thoughts of yesterday, and our present thoughts build our life of tomorrow; our life is the creation of our mind. If a man speaks or acts with an impure mind, suffering follows him as the wheel of suffering follows the beast that draws the cart.	*You make yourself for yourself. Nothing outside makes your choices for you or decides what the consequences of those choices will be. What you think leads to what you do and what you do leads to inevitable consequences.*
2 What we are today comes from our thoughts of yesterday, and our present thoughts build our life of tomorrow; our life is the creation of our mind. If a man speaks or acts with a pure mind, joy follows him as his own shadow.	*Right thinking will lead to right action and the avoidance of suffering.*
3 'He insulted me, he hurt me, he defeated me, he robbed me.' Those who think such thoughts will not be free of hate.	*There's no point in trying to get revenge on those who do you harm. Two wrongs don't make a right. You must let go of your anger even if it is justified.*
4 'He insulted me, he hurt me, he defeated me, he robbed me.' Those who do not think such thoughts will be free of hate.	*Hatred clings to you and harms you. You must detach yourself from it and it will no longer fuel your misery.*
5 For hate is not conquered by hate: hate is conquered by love. This is a law eternal.	*Hatred leads to more hatred. Love is a better response towards those who have wronged you.*

6 Many do not know that we are here in this world to live in harmony. Those who do not know this fight against each other.	*People are ignorant of the true nature of things. If we do not see the connections between ourselves and all living beings then we will not act with compassion. We act with compassion when we realise that every living thing deserves to be treated compassionately.*
7 He who lives only for pleasures, and whose soul is not in harmony, who considers not the food he eats, is idle and has not the power of virtue – such a man is moved by Mara, is moved by selfish temptations, even as a weak tree is shaken by the wind.	*People live in the short-term and for themselves. By living for pleasure, you might get immediate 'reward' but ultimately you're doing the wrong thing for others and for yourself.*
8 But he who lives not for pleasures, and whose soul is in self-harmony, who eats or fasts with moderation, and has faith and the power of virtue – this man is not moved by temptations, as a great rock is not shaken by the wind.	*Self-control is one of the keys to living well – not being shaken or even stirred by temptations. This is the right way to live.*
9 If a man puts on a pure yellow robe with a soul which is impure, without self-harmony and truth, he is not worthy of the holy yellow robe.	*Your living the good life has to be real. There's no point in putting on a robe and pretending to be good. You must actually do the right thing, not just look as if you are. (There is a pun here as the word for yellow is closely linked to the word for purity… but the connection is lost in the translation.)*
10 But he who is pure from sin and whose soul is strong in virtue, who has self-harmony and truth, he is worthy of the holy yellow robe.	*Rewards only mean something when you truly deserve them.*
11 Those who think the unreal is, and think the Real is not, they shall never reach the Truth, lost in the path of wrong thought.	*If you live in ignorance you will never gain Enlightenment. People sometimes live topsy-turvy lives. We have to put our lives right to stand a chance of reaching the Truth.*
12 But those who know the Real is, and know the unreal is not, they shall indeed reach the Truth, safe on the path of right thought.	*If you're walking in the dark you can't see and you're likely to fall over and hurt yourself. Wake up and open your eyes! Those who walk in the light will finish their journey safely.*
13 Even as rain breaks through an ill-thatched house, passions will break through an ill-guarded mind.	*You may think that you are protected, but if you do not pay attention to your thoughts, then evil thoughts will creep in and you'll end up doing what is wrong.*
14 But even as rain breaks not through a well-thatched house, passions will not break through a well-guarded mind.	*Self-control again. Keep your own house in order and you'll be safe from life's assaults.*

Dhammapada 90–99

Dhammapada text	Commentary
90 There is no suffering for him who has finished his journey, and abandoned grief, who has freed himself on all sides, and thrown off all fetters.	*The attainment of Nibbana snuffs out all suffering and grief. Fetters tie you down; Nibbana – the attainment of Enlightenment – sets you free.*
91 The mindful depart with their thoughts well-collected, they are not happy in their abode; like swans who have left their lake, they leave their house and home.	*Nibbana leaves everything behind. It is when you become one with Reality and cease to be.*
92 Men who have no riches, who live on recognised food, who have perceived void and unconditioned freedom (Nibbana), their path is difficult to understand, like that of birds in the air.	*You can describe flying but you can't really communicate what it means for the bird because you can't experience it in the way they do. So, Nibbana can't be described, only experienced. Also, you can't describe where a bird has flown – it has been there but there is nothing obviously there to trace its path.*
93 He whose appetites are stilled, who is not absorbed in enjoyment, who has perceived void and unconditioned freedom (Nibbana), his path is difficult to understand, like that of birds in the air.	*The spiritual freedom of the Enlightened is like the flight path of a bird. Just as a bird moves in flight without putting its feet on the earth – so too does the Enlightened being move forwards (symbolically, of course).*
94 The gods even envy him whose senses, like horses well broken in by the driver, have been subdued, who is free from pride, and free from appetites.	*The senses need to be controlled – otherwise they will take over and take us for a ride. They must be kept in their place to help progress towards Nibbana.*
95 Such a one who does his duty is tolerant like the earth, like Indra's bolt; he is like a lake without mud; no new births are in store for him.	*Freeing oneself from earthly attachment is the key – 'the mud in the waters' settles and everything becomes clear. This clarity leads to an end to rebirth and escape from the cycle of Samsara. The lake represents serenity and purity.*
96 His thought is quiet, quiet are his word and deed, when he has obtained freedom by true knowledge, when he has thus become a quiet man.	*When the waters of life are still and clear, ignorance (which is the mud making the water difficult to see in) is gone and peace is achieved. This leads to a person who is 'quiet', that is, contented and free from attachment, and therefore Enlightened.*
97 The man who is free from credulity, but knows the uncreated, who has cut all ties, removed all temptations, renounced all desires, he is the greatest of men.	*The Enlightened person has no attachments to anything and has escaped from the problems associated with desire. Cutting yourself off like this is the way to Nibbana.*

98 In a hamlet or in a forest, in the deep water or on the dry land, wherever venerable persons (Arhanta) dwell, that place is delightful.	*Remember that Arhats attain Enlightenment and remain alive – they don't attain Nibbana only after physical death. Obviously where the Arhats are is a place of peace.*
99 Forests are delightful; where the world finds no delight, there the passionless will find delight, for they look not for pleasures.	*Following Enlightenment, a person will not seek the same things as the unenlightened – so their concept of pleasure will be different from everyone else's.*

Textual work

The following is the kind of exam question you may meet in your RMPS exam. **Remember**, there are no prescribed sources at **Intermediate 1**.

Read the following source, then answer all of the parts of the question (a)–(e). The number of marks available for each part is indicated; use them to help you answer the question.

Dhammapada 7

'He who lives only for pleasures, and whose soul is not in harmony, who considers not the food he eats, is idle and has not the power of virtue – such a man is moved by Mara, is moved by selfish temptations, even as a weak tree is shaken by the wind.'

(a) Who or what is Mara?   *(1KU)*

(b) What role does Mara play in the story of the Buddha?   *(4KU)*

(c) This source goes on to describe the kind of person who will be able to avoid such temptations, the Arhat. What do Buddhists mean by an Arhat?   *(4KU, 4AE)*

(d) Why is Enlightenment a goal for Buddhists?   *(2KU, 6AE)*

(e) This text goes on to explain the importance of 'the well-guarded mind'. Why is it important for Buddhists to have a well-guarded mind?   *(2KU, 2AE)*

(25 marks)

You get a brand new games machine – the 'PlayBay'. It's the machine of your dreams. (You can even play 'Nibbana'™ on it!) You've wanted this games console for ages. You've saved up and sacrificed all sorts of other possible purchases. And now you have it – it's wonderful, amazing, incredible. You walk along the street playing it, oblivious to everything else until, out of the corner of your eye, you notice something in a shop window... Could it be? Surely not? Yes it is! It's the 'PlayBay 2'!!! You must have it...

Are people ever going to be happy? How are we going to become happy?

By now you know the kind of answers given by Buddhists to the questions, 'What is being a human all about?' and 'What are we aiming for in life?' Now let's tackle the last remaining question: 'How do we achieve these aims?'

We put a lot of energy into trying to obtain the things we want in life, but what is it we are looking for, what do we want the achievements to give us? Probably one of the reasons you are doing RMPS is that you like thinking things through for yourself. Pupils doing some subjects at school are happy to be told what to write ('Just tell me the answer, please!'), whereas in a subject like RMPS you have to think things through to find the answers. So far you have thought about what

Buddhists think is wrong with life and what we should be aiming for. Now it's time to think about how do we get there? Is there an easy answer to this?

Again, different Buddhist groups have different approaches to the issue of how we get from life what we're meant to. There is no one answer, but there are common ideas throughout Buddhism. As you already know, in Buddhism, beliefs should be linked to actions. You can't just think loving kindness and compassion – you have to do it too. Remember, beliefs and actions are two parts of the Fourth Noble Truth.

Before we consider how to do this, however, let's summarise what you have learned so far from this course:

◆ The Human Condition – living things suffer because we are unenlightened. This leads to us being ignorant of the fact that everything is impermanent including ourselves. Our suffering is caused by craving something which, in our ignorance, we don't know isn't real.

◆ The Goals – the aim of existence is to make progress towards Enlightenment and eventually to attain Nibbana, which is the cessation of all suffering caused by existence.

How we achieve our goals – The Means – is covered in this section.

Getting into it

◆ How do you get what you want in life?

◆ What beliefs do you hold?

◆ How central are these beliefs in your life?

◆ How do these beliefs lead to action?

◆ What action?

◆ How public and open are you about what you believe?

◆ Have you ever taken part in or witnessed ceremonies where people demonstrate what they believe?

◆ What kind of world are you helping to create?

◆ What things in life do you think are unfair or unjust?

◆ Do you fight against what you think is unfair or unjust?

◆ What groups are you part of?

◆ How do these groups help you in life?

The Three Jewels

My bedroom
My granny's kitchen
My best friend
My football club
TV
The quiet little place at the bottom of the garden
My big brother
The seaside
A forest in the drizzle
The shops
A busy street where no one knows me
A really good book
Shut off from the world on my iPod

Refuge

Taking refuge

To become a Buddhist all you need to do is to recite the following:

I take refuge in the Buddha
I take refuge in the Dhamma
I take refuge in the Sangha.

When did you last need to turn to someone or something for support? When did you last feel the need to get away from it all? At difficult times in our lives we sometimes look for refuge – a place or a person who helps us make sense of things which aren't easy to make sense of. Your refuge might be quite different from anyone else's. It might be a place which is special to you, somewhere where you can be yourself, or somewhere where the pressures of life are just a little easier. Your refuge might be a person – someone you look up to, someone who is strong, someone who can show you the way. Or your refuge might be a group – people you feel comfortable with, people who give you a sense of belonging or community.

Time Out

18

Where's your refuge?

For Buddhists, the three refuges – the Buddha, the Dhamma and the Sangha (the Buddhist community) – help them make sense of life. These 'Three Jewels' point them in the right direction along the road to Nibbana. They also help them practically to cope with the inevitable suffering which life involves.

The Buddha

Why is the Buddha a refuge?

◆ He is a role model: his life and behaviour while alive set Buddhists an example of how they should live.

◆ His teaching lives on after his death showing people how they should live.

◆ The Buddha's Enlightenment shows people that they can be Enlightened too, and so escape the endless cycle of births and rebirths.

◆ As the founder of the faith, he initiated all the benefits Buddhism brings to its followers. Buddhists believe that the Buddha set in motion a chain of events which, if understood, can lead everyone to Enlightenment.

◆ Because of this you're free from avoidable mental suffering, not ordinary inevitable suffering.

After the Buddha's Enlightenment, he taught for many years until his death and gathered followers around him. He showed them the Middle Way to Enlightenment and encouraged them to spread this message around, bringing Enlightenment to as many beings as possible. About 500 years after his death they grouped together and started writing down the things he said before they all forgot them. Also, stories from the Buddha's previous lives (that is, before he was born as Siddartha Gautama) also form part of the teachings of Buddhism. Buddhists also learn helpful things about life, the universe and everything from these stories.

A Buddha as teacher

A Buddha is thus not merely an Enlightened One, but is above all an Enlightener, a World Teacher. His function is to rediscover, in an age of spiritual darkness, the lost path to Nirvana, to perfect spiritual freedom, and teach this path to the world at large. Thereby others can follow in his steps and arrive at the same experience of emancipation that he himself achieved. A Buddha is not unique in attaining Nirvana.

Source: www.purifymind.com/BuddhaMessage.htm

THE MEANS

The Mahayana and Theravada schools have slightly different views about what happened to the Buddha after death. For the Theravada, he passed into final Nibbana. The Mahayana, however, thought the Buddha wouldn't leave them entirely on their own. They thought he was such a compassionate being that he would remain in contact with them in some way to help them. They came up with the idea of the Buddha having three 'bodies' (Trikaya):

◆ an earthly body (Nirmanakaya): the physical body he occupied on Earth (your standard human body)

◆ a heavenly body (Sambhogakaya): a perfected spiritual existence in a kind of perfected heavenly realm

◆ a 'transcendent' body (Dharmakaya): the Buddha as something which has itself become the ultimate Truth.

These differences between Mahayana and Theravadin teachings are minor issues. The important thing to know is that a refuge is something in which you find comfort and understanding. All Buddhists find this in the Buddha.

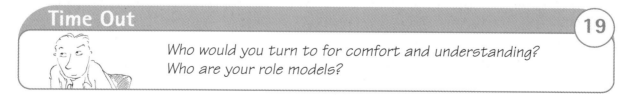

Time Out

19

Who would you turn to for comfort and understanding? Who are your role models?

The Dhamma

Why is the Dhamma a refuge?

◆ The Dhamma is the written record of the Buddha's teaching. Buddha taught his disciples by speaking to them, not by writing books or scribbling things down. His words would have been lost if they hadn't been written down by his followers at some point after his death. These writings became the scriptures of Buddhism.

◆ The Dhamma is also the whole collection of Buddhism's teachings. Remember that Buddhism is also about practice, and so the Dhamma includes more than just the direct teachings of the Buddha. There are now many written sources

of Buddhist belief, as well as many Buddhists who pass on to others their understanding of what the faith means and what the Buddha meant. Both of these help Buddhists to know what is the right thing to do to progress towards and eventually achieve Nibbana. Buddhism stresses the importance of learning not just from sacred texts and the teachings of those long gone, but also from those who are living and the example of their lives. Remember that in Buddhism, the Enlightened are thought of as walking among us – as Arhats or Bodhisattvas. These beings are able to teach the Dhamma just like the historical Buddha did.

• The Dhamma is the Buddhist way of life. This means that it isn't just words – it is also actions, beliefs, how you speak, and so on. Every moral choice you make has either good or bad Kammic consequences. The Dhamma can also be thought of as the Middle Way (or path) of Buddhism that leads to Enlightenment.

The Dhamma 1

The most wonderful thing about all these massive instructions [the dhamma], both in theory and practical aspects, is that it can be verified at any time by any able person who will steadfastly practise with Nibbana as the ultimate goal and realises the Truths and joins the exclusive membership of Enlightened Beings (Ariya persons) even in this very life.

Source: web.ukonline.co.uk/buddhism/tipitaka.htm

Talk Point

What do you use to guide you through life?

Theravada and Mahayana Buddhists have slightly different views on what is and isn't Dhamma and how important the different kinds of Dhamma are.

The Tripitaka

The Theravada school of Buddhism thinks of itself as the one which adheres most closely to the teachings of the Buddha as they originally were passed on. It stresses the importance of the Tripitaka. This is thought of as three baskets, each of which contains an important part of the Dhamma. The three baskets are:

◆ the Vinaya pitaka: this contains the set of formal rules for monks and nuns, telling them about the Buddha's teachings, mainly on physical things. It's like a rule book of do's and don'ts with accompanying punishments.

◆ the Sutta pitaka: this contains more complete explanations by the Buddha of what his teachings are about, helping to make sure that people clearly understand the meaning of what he said.

◆ Abhidhamma pitaka – this is more theoretical than practical. It is sometimes thought of as the higher teaching or more philosophical teaching.

The Mahayana Buddhists also believe in the Tripitaka, but they also accept Buddhist teachings which didn't come straight from the Buddha, but came from people's understanding of what he said. Remember that the idea of skilful actions means that Buddhists should apply the teachings of the faith in a way that is suitable for the individual person and for the situation. This means that the Dhamma should never be thought of as a collection of writings which you have to accept slavishly, letter by letter. This is partly what leads Mahayana Buddhists to find their lessons in Buddhism wherever they can.

The Dhamma as a signpost

It is very important to understand that the Dhamma isn't like the sacred scriptures in some other world religions – it is not worshipped or treated as an end in itself. The Dhamma isn't thought of as the source of Enlightenment – it just indicates the way. Sometimes the Dhamma is compared to a raft (which could help you escape a desert island). The raft gets you where you want to go, but isn't important in itself.

For Buddhists, the Dhamma isn't the destination; rather, it's a sign pointing towards the destination. The Dhamma helps you to find your way and make sense of life so it acts as a refuge both from life's confusion and from the fact of life's illusion. What is **written** is not as important as what is **meant**. The Buddha is often spoken of as setting the wheel in motion – in other words of starting people on the road to Enlightenment. The Dhamma is the collection of road signs along the way.

The Dhamma 2

Dhamma also has a practical sense, something applicable to our own life. Dhamma is that which sustains us, which supports us, or which upholds our own effort to live in virtue and goodness. In this sense Dhamma is the path. On the one hand it is the lower path of virtue, on the other, Dhamma is the Supramundane path, the higher path that leads to realisation of the true nature of things.

Source: www.beyondthenet.net/dhamma/s_dhamma_.htm

The Sangha

Why is the Sangha a refuge?

◆ The Sangha is the community of Buddhists. Almost all of us like to be part of a group. Buddhism is sometimes seen as a very individual religion, but that's not really the case. Buddhists support each other and learn from each other, just like any other group of people. When you share beliefs and a way of life with others it keeps you strong in your beliefs and practice. You can get support when you need it and do the same for others in your community.

The Sangha

◆ There are two main groups in the Sangha: the laity and the ordained (in the Western Buddhist Order there are ordained Buddhists who are neither lay nor monastic). The laity is just ordinary people who may work and live next door to you. They don't wear any special clothes, but do follow the Buddhist way of life, whether very strictly or quite loosely. The ordained are monks and nuns (bhikkus and bhikkunis). Some live a monastic life and have no contact with the outside world, while others, also living in monastic communities, work in the local community helping people in various ways. As a monk or nun you take on special rules and restrictions in your life. All of these should help you in your progress towards Enlightenment. You might also adopt particular ways of dressing and presenting yourself to the world, such as shaving your head. One of the reasons for doing this is that it helps you detach yourself from thinking about how you look and what others think about how you look. This helps you become detached generally and so realise that nothing stays the same. (After all, your hair will eventually become old, wiry and grey one day!). Also, instead of wasting your time and energy on unimportant things such as personal appearance, you will be able to focus more on progressing towards Nibbana.

THE MEANS

◆ Within the Sangha, there is a subgroup of people called the AryaSangha. These are the 'crack troops' of Buddhism – the Enlightened beings (Bodhisattvas for Mahayans and Arhats for Theravadins).

Mahayana and Theravada Buddhists also think about the Sangha differently. Mahayana Buddhists stress that everyone can become a Bodhisattva, whereas in the Theravada school it's far more likely that you'll become an Arhat if you are a monk or nun. If you're a lay Theravadin, then you're more likely to be aiming for a better rebirth next time which might enable you to become a monk or nun. This is a bit simplistic though, because in Tibetan Buddhism (which is a specific branch of the Mahayana tradition) there's a strict hierarchy of monks and lay people right up to one of the top men, the Dalai Lama. (Interestingly, the Dalai Lama always refers to himself as 'just a humble monk' while his followers think of him as the Bodhisattva Avalokiteshvara.)

Time Out

(20)

Which groups are you a part of? Why are you part of these groups? What do you give to them and what do you get from them?

An Interview with a Mahayana monk

The interviewed monk is 50 years old, grew up in Birmingham and has been ordained for 14 years.

Q1. Why did you get ordained?
'It seemed like a good idea at the time!'

Q2. How does your family feel about it?
'At first they were not sure, but later they came to see the benefits of my life and how I am helping others, they became very supportive and very proud actually.'

Q3. Do you miss your old life?
'No actually, not in the slightest!'

4. What do you like most about being a monk or a nun?
'Freedom! Freedom from the everyday hassles that lay people have to go through.'

In some Buddhist countries, lay people become monks and nuns and remain so for ever. In other Buddhist countries, you can become a temporary monk or nun and then go back to 'normal' life. In some countries this is often the only way in which some young people can get any education.

As a monk or nun you take on strict rules for living. Some Buddhists find this too hard, so they adopt a 'middle way' – living a 'normal' life with families and jobs, but taking on some (but not all) of the stricter rules. There's nothing wrong with this selective approach; it's just a good example of skilful actions in practice!

The FWBO's view of refuge

Around the path to Enlightenment taught by the Buddha have developed numerous religious forms, institutions, and cultural practices. While these may be means through which individuals can follow the Buddha's path, Sangharakshita [the founder of FWBO] suggests that sometimes the forms have become ends in themselves. What matters is the inner commitment.

The task for Buddhists today is to discern what in the Buddhist tradition genuinely does support going for Refuge, and then to put it into practice in their lives.

Source: www.fwbo.org/fwbo/principles.html

In the West, you can become a member of many lay Buddhist organisations like the Friends of the Western Buddhist Order (FWBO). The FWBO began as a way of following Buddhism without having to take on an 'Eastern' way of life, for example, dressing like a Tibetan monk or learning Pali or Sanskrit in order to understand the scriptures. The emphasis for FWBO is on living according to the teachings of the Buddha and adapting these according to the situation and the person. Even here you can be a completely lay person or you can be a slightly more involved lay person – you can even be an 'ordained lay person' where you take on special restrictions and wear a special item (kesa) while not having to be a fully ordained monk or nun. Order members do not think of themselves as lay Buddhists, they're neither monk or lay.

THE MEANS

Talk Point

Why do you think some people feel it is necessary to dress and behave in 'Eastern' ways when they become Buddhists? What do you think of it?

In addition to organisations such as the FWBO, places like the Samye Ling Temple in Dumfriesshire also have a mixture of lay people and monks and nuns. Such lay people might do the jobs that the monks and nuns can't do (because these jobs mean doing things that break monastic rules, for example, handling money). This mixed structure allows the monastic community to continue to do its work – for everyone's benefit.

For many Buddhists today, whether in the East or West, the Sangha is the worldwide community of Buddhists. In fact, it is anyone who has stated that they want to take refuge in the Three Jewels. And as a member of the Sangha, whether lay or ordained, you can take on different levels of rules to live by. But one thing which is not really up for discussion is whether you accept the Fourth Noble Truth or not, because that is at the very heart of the faith.

Activities

Knowledge, Understanding, Evaluation

1 Describe one place which you think of as a refuge.

2 How might the Buddha's teaching 'live on'?

3 In what ways is the Buddha a role model?

4 What is the function of a Buddha, according to the extract from the purifymind.com website?

5 What three forms do Mahayana Buddhists think the Buddha takes?

6 What three things count as the Dhamma?

7 In what way does the extract from the ukonline.co.uk website suggest that the Dhamma isn't all that unique?

8 What is the Abhidhamma pitaka?

9 What the main difference between the Theravada and Mahayana views about the Dhamma?

10 Why might a Buddhist describe the Dhamma as a signpost?

11 What point is the extract from the beyondthenet.net website making about the Dhamma?

12 Why do people like to be part of groups?

13 What special things can being part of a religious group give you?

14 What is the difference between the lay and monastic community in Buddhism?

15 Why might a Buddhist shave his head?

16 What do Theravadins think is one of the major benefits of being a monk or nun?

17 What does the founder of the FWBO think of many religious practices?

18 In what ways does the FWBO try to make Buddhism more relevant to our way of life in the West?

19 How do you think the monastic community can help the lay community?

20 How do you think the lay community can help the monastic community?

21 Why do you think people become monks and nuns?

Practical Activities

1 Make up a display board with the word REFUGE at the centre. Illustrate examples of the word from people in the class and from Buddhism.

2 Bearing in mind what you have learned about Buddhism to this point, what would you ask the Buddha if you could? Write a list of questions and pass them to someone else in the class who will try to answer them.

3 Find an example of the written Dhamma on the Internet. If you can find an audio version, listen to it too. The Dhamma as scripture isn't always in the forms of books. Describe how it is written and stored and what it sounds like when read.

4 Read more the interviews with monks and nuns at:
www.dharmaforkids.com/Sangha/monks/monks.htm#
Make a report on the interviews. Try to arrange for a monk to come into your school for an interview.

Unit Assessment Question

Int 2 In what ways is the Buddha a refuge?   *(4)*

Higher

How do the Mahayana and Theravada schools of Buddhism differ in their views about monks and nuns?   *(6)*

Sample Exam Question

Int 2 'The Buddha is the most important of the three refuges of Buddhism.' Would a Buddhist agree? Give reasons for your answer.   *(6AE)*

Higher

'The Dhamma is the source of Enlightenment.' Would all Buddhists agree?   *(4KU, 6AE)*

Homework

Find out about a typical day in the life of a Buddhist monk or nun. Write an imaginary diary entry for such a day.

Personal Reflection

When someone becomes a monk or nun they have to give up many things from their old way of life. However, they always say that the benefits of being a monk or nun outweigh that. What would you find hard to give up? What would you be expecting in return?

The Noble Eightfold Path

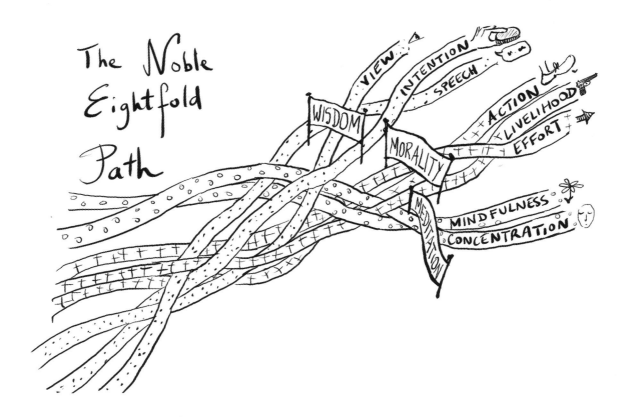

The Fourth Noble Truth

The Buddha's final Noble Truth – the Noble Eightfold Path – describes a way of escaping the suffering expressed by the first three Noble Truths, answering the questions they pose. It was a practical response to the fact of suffering and the cause of suffering – craving. The aim of life, remember, is to escape suffering and attain Enlightenment. The way to do this in practice is to follow a set of guiding principles for life. These guiding principles should cover everything in life – every eventuality and every problem. They are a way of looking at life as well as a way of dealing with it.

The Noble Eightfold Path should be followed as a way of avoiding extremes. This Middle Way of the Buddha means that you should avoid having too much or too little of anything – instead you should have everything in moderation.

Consider money as an example. Having too little money obviously makes your life hard. You can't get the things you need, not even the basics, and you spend too much time worrying about how to survive. On the other hand, having too much money might have its problems too – you might spend all your time worrying about the safety of your wealth, or even the safety of your family. You might wonder if your friends are friends because they like you or because they like your money. So, having too much or too little money can be a problem. Something in the middle is probably best.

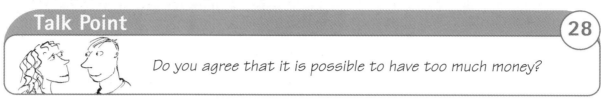

Talk Point

Do you agree that it is possible to have too much money?

(28)

No doubt the Buddha realised that his followers would want specifics about ***how*** to live the right life rather than just ***why*** they should live the right life. This is what the Noble Eightfold Path aims to do.

Eight Paths to Nibbana – made of three kinds of brick!

Sometimes the Noble Eightfold Path is taught as being like a set of steps, but this doesn't describe it accurately. There's no order or sequence, where one element comes before or after another. It is better to think of it is made up of eight separate paths, which cross over sometimes on the way, all leading to Nibbana. The paths of the Noble Eightfold Path are organised into three groups, which are known as the Threefold Way. You could think of each of the Threefold Ways as a type of brick which goes to make up the Eightfold Path. The Noble Eightfold Path and the Threefold Way can be summarised in this way:

◆ Right View
◆ Right Intention   } Wisdom
◆ Right Action

◆ Right Livelihood
◆ Right Effort   } Morality
◆ Right Speech

◆ Right Mindfulness   } Meditation
◆ Right Concentration

Wisdom (Prajna)

◆ Right View or Understanding

◆ Right Intention

◆ Right Speech

The first three paths show **wisdom**, which is linking thoughts to actions. This isn't really about learning Buddhism or even the teaching of the Buddha; rather, it's about finding things out for yourself. Remember that Buddhists believe that you can work out the Dhamma for yourself. You can use the formal teachings of Buddhism to help you do this, but you have only really achieved it when you have experienced it for yourself. True wisdom has to be found within you.

> ### Time Out 21
>
> *What do you think makes a person wise?*

Morality (Sila)

◆ Right Action

◆ Right Livelihood

◆ Right Effort

These three parts of the path show **morality**, which also puts beliefs into action. There's no one morality, no one way of doing the right thing. This is because of the idea of 'skilful actions', that is, what is right is linked to the person and the situation and the right thing to do might be completely different depending upon the person or situation. There are specific rules about right and wrong in Buddhism, but these too simply point to the need to live life applying the principle of skilful actions, showing loving kindness and compassion.

> ### Talk Point 29
>
> *How do you decide what's right and wrong?*

Meditation (Samadhi)

◆ Right Mindfulness

◆ Right Concentration

These two parts of the Path show **meditation.** This doesn't just mean sitting cross-legged; it is a whole way of training your mind to see things as they really are. For Buddhists, if your mind isn't right, then your actions won't be either. This is linked to the important Buddhist idea of awareness. The whole of the Buddha's teaching, after all, was about becoming aware of the way things really are rather than the way they seem to be. Once you have this awareness you're on the right road to Enlightenment. Enlightenment itself is awareness of the true nature of Reality.

THE MEANS

Time Out

Can you think of a time when your mind 'wasn't in the right place'? What effects on your behaviour did this have?

Examples of the Eightfold Path

None of the Eightfold Paths exists in isolation – each is linked to all the others in one way or another. Let's look at four of them as examples of what they mean in theory and practice.

Right Intention (Samma sankappa)

This takes us back to Mr Bongle and Mr Bungle – what made their actions good or bad? Intention was part of it. If you mean something bad to happen then that's just as bad as if you made the bad thing actually happen. An intention can be wrong in itself, because it creates a state of mind from which it's more likely that negative things will flow than positive ones. Most evil things come from evil ideas, and similarly most good things come from good thinking. The state of mind creates the world outside and so making sure that your intentions are good is vital for the Buddhist.

Buddha taught that there were three kinds of Right Intention:

1   The intention to resist desire. We all want things, but sometimes we also want to want them. Think of 'fashion victims' – they wear the latest fashions (even though some people think it makes them look very silly) both because they want to and because they want other people to see that they are doing so. The process of weaning yourself off desiring things has to begin with *wanting* not to want things – that has to be your first intention. This kind of intention is linked to the renunciation of what is unreal.

2   The intention to show good will. We could achieve the intention to resist desire and stop there. What good would that be? It would be the same as cutting yourself off from things with nothing positive to replace them. It would be the difference between going on a diet where you eat nothing (which harms your body and makes you grumpy) to going on a diet where you replace chips and burgers with fruit and salad (gives you energy and makes you feel good about yourself). The Right Intention means not only

resisting what's bad but seeking what's good. This kind of intention is linked to loving kindness (Metta).

3 The intention to act on that good will. You can think good thoughts, but if they don't become good actions, then they don't serve much purpose. Right Intention has to be followed through with right action. It's no good meaning well but doing nothing. This kind of intention is closely linked to compassion (Karuna).

Talk Point 30

Is it enough to 'mean well'?

Right Intention

Right Intent means persistence and a passion for the journey. Setting out to climb a high mountain means you must understand the lay of the land and the pitfalls, the other team members, and the equipment you need. This is similar to Right Understanding. But you will only climb the mountain if you really want to and have a passion for the climb. This is Right Intent. The mountain we climb here is our journey though life.

Source: www.acay.com.au/~silkroad/buddha/p_path.htm

Right Speech (Samma vaca)

Speech is one of the things which separates humans from all other living things. Speech is the power of conveying what is in your mind into someone else's mind – it's one of the ways we communicate ideas and emotions, whether both positive or negative. Despite the belief that 'sticks and stones may break my bones but names will never hurt me', this just isn't true. Words can build up or knock down. They can very quickly lead to love or hate. They can be just as powerful as anything else to make us feel great or make us feel miserable.

Communication

And what is it all about? What is being communicated with this deluge of words? Much of it is telling us what to think, what to wear, what to eat, what to read, what we should look like and what will make us happy. Much of it is trying to persuade us of one thing or another – who to vote for, what to buy. And much of it amounts to the empty prattle of radio DJs or the equally empty content of huge swathes of the mass media. And what is spoken and written in the world around us enters into our own consciousness and becomes the content of our own conversation too. The banality of most verbal communication is not a new thing, it is just the vast quantity available to us that's new. But verbal communication will always be as mediocre or as profound as the hearts and minds that provide its content and expression.

Source: ratnaghosa.fwbo.net/wordone.html

THE MEANS

Time Out

1   Is there too much 'empty speech' around today?

2   How do you think Right Speech relates to other forms of human communication?

23

The Buddha (who taught through the spoken word rather than the written word) said there were four features of Right Speech:

1   To avoid false speech, that is, lying. (Although the notion of skilful actions may permit white lies when the occasion is appropriate.) Imagine a society where it was normal for people sometimes to tell the truth and sometimes to lie – you would never know what was going on. Society works best when we assume that most people tell the truth most of the time.

2   To avoid using words as weapons against others. Think of the last time you wanted to be really nasty to someone. You probably started off by thinking of the worst name you could call the person! This also means not using words to question something about someone (like their honesty, for example). It also means not using words to damage someone's reputation or put them in a negative light. Speech like this is motivated by badness and leads to even more badness. Instead, speech should be used to create harmony.

3   To avoid hurtful words. The previous two examples aren't always as direct as this one. This is where you use words with the specific intention of hurting someone. It can be avoided by demonstrating patience – even in the most difficult situations.

4   To avoid gossip and pointless chatter ('empty words'). Words should be positive and speech uplifting. Words should be gentle and supportive. Some modern Buddhists believe 'pointless chatter' applies also to TV, radio, cinema, and so on, because they take your mind off what's real and make you empty-headed.

Obviously, swearing is prohibited, but Right Speech isn't so much about what we shouldn't do as what we should. What we say reveals what we think and can lead to what we do – everything is tied to something else. Our speech, like the Buddha's, should be used carefully to lead ourselves and others towards Nibbana and away from ignorance.

Right Action (Samma kamanta)

Again, the concept of Right Action stresses that Buddhism is definitely not about sitting around all day 'contemplating'. As you know, what you do and how you live your life has Kammic consequences – for you and others – including setting up your patterns for rebirth minute by minute. There are three categories of Right Action:

1 To avoid harming living things. This means all living things as far as possible, but most definitely conscious beings (although it is not always easy to work out the difference). Again, harming things suggests bad motives (and so bad intentions); it can lead to revenge and the overall increase of bad things in the world. Instead, the Buddhist should have compassion for all things because they're all engaged in trying to escape from the wheel of Samsara.

2 To avoid taking what is not given. Stealing is an obvious example of this, but it also means holding things back from people who should rightly have them. Examples include photocopying bits of a book (to avoid paying for it), and not telling someone about something which could be theirs if only they knew about it. The motivation behind stealing is obviously wrong and it too can lead to a downwards spiral and an increase of badness in the world. Any action where you knowingly deprive someone of something which belongs to them counts as taking what's not given, and this is bad Kamma indeed.

Help!

3 Avoiding sexual misconduct. The easiest way to avoid sexual misconduct is, as you would expect, not to have sex at all. That's how most monks and nuns deal with this category. The link between sex and desire is obvious, especially in contemporary society. Since Buddhism is about resisting desire, it might seem logical that its teaching would advocate complete abstinence. However, there is some freedom about how this is understood, especially since Buddhism is all about what feels right for each individual. The most important

principle underlying Buddhism's approach to sex and sexual misconduct is that, no matter what the details are, sexual relationships should avoid harming others in any way.

In short, your actions are an expression of your beliefs and so, like your beliefs, they should be right if you want to attain Enlightenment.

Wholesome and unwholesome actions

Overall, one can say that an 'unwholesome' action is one that arises from greed, hatred or delusion (or a combination of these), leads to immediate suffering in others and/or oneself and thus to further karmic suffering for oneself in the future, and contributes to more unwholesome states arising and to liberating wisdom being weakened. 'Wholesome' actions have the opposite characteristics. They arise from a state of mind which is virtuous, as judged by the action's motive and the agent's knowledge of likely harm or benefit, its contribution to the improvement of the character of the person who does it, and thus its assistance in moving a person along the path to Nirvana.

Source: jbe.gold.ac.uk/2/harvey.html

Time Out

24

Are some kinds of stealing worse than others? Compare murder with stealing a banana from someone's lunch box, or robbing a bank with fiddling your taxes.

Right Livelihood (Samma avija)

This means earning your living in a way which matches up with the other ideas of the Eightfold Path. So you have to earn your living, honestly, legally, peacefully and without causing direct or indirect harm to living things. Obviously, this is the practical application of many of the ideals of the Eightfold Path – those covering Right Action and Intentions and so on. There are a number of things to avoid if you want to adopt a Right Livelihood:

1   Avoid working in weapons. This could be making them, selling them, designing them and so on. But it can also mean any activity related to these occupations, for example, if you had a organic vegetarian whole foods mobile kitchen which stopped by to sell products outside a factory which made bolts for tanks you might still be involved in wrong livelihood.

2   Avoid making money from the buying and selling of living beings. This could be something pretty straightforward like being a turkey farmer. It could also be something more unusual like working in the slave trade or people trafficking or something to do with prostitution.

3   Avoid working in the meat industry. By definition, the meat industry causes harm to living beings, so butchers might find it just a little tricky to be

Buddhists. (Might the principle of skilful actions allow the possibility of Buddhist butchers?)

4 Avoid working with poisons and intoxicants. An obvious example is the growing and selling of drugs and so on, but for Buddhists it would also include working in any way in the whisky industry in Scotland.

Right Livelihood

According to the FWBO, a right livelihood might involve a business observing the following:

◆ Firstly they provide a reasonable level of support for their workers, but they do not pay wages or salaries. The level of support is worked out to give people a reasonable standard of living, according to their personal circumstances and needs.

◆ Secondly they only engage in work that is ethical.

◆ Thirdly they offer a context for friendship and *kalyana mitrata*.

Source based on information at: www.fwbo.org/rightlivelihood.html

All of these categories relate in some way to the possible harm of the livelihood of other living things. Causing harm is obviously bad Kamma, but earning your living by causing harm is obviously worse. Of course, skilful action has to be factored into this, so maybe in some cases, it's not a straightforward task to label jobs as simply 'good' or 'bad'.

Talk Point (31)

How would the world change if everyone followed the principle of Right Livelihood?

The Noble Eightfold Path is simply the Buddhist way of working out the details of how to live a life which is heading towards Nibbana. It's trying to put some practical flesh on some very theoretical bones. This helps Buddhists not only to understand that life is about attaining Enlightenment but it also shows them the practical steps which they must take to get there. These guiding principles lead towards a whole way of life which is lived ethically.

Activities

Knowledge, Understanding, Evaluation

1 What is the Fourth Noble Truth?

2 What do Buddhists mean by the Middle Way?

3 What do you think of living according to a Middle Way?

4 Is having too much money as bad as having too little?

5 Why do you think the Buddha came up with the Noble Eightfold Path?

6 Where do Buddhists think you can find wisdom?

7 Is there such a thing as one unchanging 'Buddhist morality'?

8 What would a Buddhist mean by awareness?

9 How important do you think intent is when deciding if someone has acted rightly or wrongly?

10 Give an example of wanting to resist desire.

11 How is loving kindness linked to intention?

12 Why do you think Buddhists place such an emphasis on Right Speech? Is it right to do so in your opinion?

13 How could watching TV be an example of wrong speech?

14 Why is it important for us to tell the truth most of the time?

15 Why might it be important to tell a lie sometimes?

16 How can you use a word as a weapon?

17 How can you avoid using hurtful words?

18 What might a Buddhist think is wrong with gossip?

19 Why should a Buddhist avoid harming living things?

20 Do you have to physically take something to steal?

21 What evidence is there in this section that Buddhists can be quite flexible about sex?

22 According to the extract on page 124, what counts as a 'wholesome' action?

23 Give an example of wrong livelihood.

24 Why is having the right livelihood important?

Practical Activities

1 Draw a series of eight interconnecting, twisting paths. Label one end of each path with one of the names of each of the Eightfold Paths. At the other end of the same path, illustrate which part of the Eightfold Path it relates to. Now have someone else use this

information to follow and highlight the path from beginning to end

2 Use a collage of newspaper stories to illustrate the idea of Right Intention.

3 Complete a table showing Right Speech and Wrong Speech.

4 Record a series of short snippets of TV and/or radio which might illustrate the idea of 'empty words'.

5 Make an old fashioned game of 'Happy Families' with a difference. Design two sets of cards (about 20 of each), half of which illustrate Wrong Livelihood (for example, Mr Blood the Butcher) and the other half Right Livelihood (for example, Mrs Brown the Teacher). Now shuffle them and distribute them face down evenly among the players. Take turns to put one card face up. When you place an example of Right Livelihood on top of an example of Wrong Livelihood you can shout 'Nibbana!'. You then pick up all the cards on the deck. The winner is the player who ends up with all the cards (or the greatest number after a certain amount of time).

Unit Assessment Question

Int 1 Give TWO reasons why Right Livelihood is important for Buddhists.   *(4)*

Int 2 Which parts of the Noble Eightfold Path are linked to wisdom (Prajna)?   *(3)*

Higher

Describe one of the kinds of Right Intention as taught by the Buddha.   *(4)*

Sample Exam Question

Int 1 'Right Speech is more about what you do say than what you don't.' Would a Buddhist agree? Give TWO reasons for your answer.   *(4AE)*

Int 2 Why should Buddhists practise Right Action?   *(2KU, 2AE)*

Higher

'Morality is the most central of the Threefold Way.' Would all Buddhists agree?   *(4KU, 6AE)*

Homework

Think about the career you want to follow after school. In what ways is it an example of Right Livelihood? What kinds of things could you do in that job to make it closer to the ideal of Right Livelihood? If you haven't got a definite career in mind, think about the job done by someone you know.

Personal Reflection

Which of the parts of the Noble Eightfold Path do you think you follow already without even thinking about it? How would you need to adjust your life so it is closer to the Noble Eightfold Path? Do you think that following the Noble Eightfold Path might improve your life?

Buddhist Ethics: The Five Precepts

A monk's song (well, kind of)
(Sung to the tune of Monty Python's 'I'm a Lumberjack' song)

Monk: I'm a yellow hat* and I'm OK
I sleep all night, meditate all day
I do not hurt, I do not kill
Nor harm in any way

Chorus: He does not hurt, he does not kill, nor harm in any way

Monk: I'm a yellow hat and I'm OK
I sleep all night, contemplate all day
I do not steal, I do not nick,
Nor take your things away

Chorus: He does not steal, he does not nick, nor take our things away

Monk: I'm a yellow hat and I'm OK
I sleep all night, ruminate all day
I do not swear, I don't tell lies
Nor gossip come what may

Chorus: He doesn't swear, he doesn't lie, nor gossip come what may

Monk: I'm a yellow hat and I'm OK
I sleep all night, ponder things all day
I don't have sex, of any kind
Nor even think that way

Chorus: He has no sex, of any kind, nor even thinks that way

Monk: I'm a yellow hat and I'm OK
I sleep all night, cogitate all day
I don't take drugs, I do not smoke
Nor booze until I sway

Chorus: He don't do drugs, he doesn't smoke, and you won't see him sway...

* A yellow hat (gelugpa) is a Tibetan Buddhist monk. The yellow hats began in the 14th century after religious reforms. There are also 'red hats' whose religious practices are very close to the Bon religion which existed in Tibet before Buddhism developed there.

Why Buddhists need ethics

Why does anyone need ethics? Doing what is right and avoiding what is wrong is central to humanity. Whereas other religions follow the commands of a God, Buddhism has to work out what's best from within. Doing the right thing is good for you for all sorts of reasons – it makes you feel good and makes others think well of you. It also makes the world a nicer place to live and that's good for you too. Doing the right thing is obviously right for the thing you do the right thing to or for. Again this is right for all sorts of reasons. In Buddhism there is the added dimension of Kamma. Your actions create the reborn you all the time. No one is judging what you do, but by the Kammic laws of cause and effect it has important consequences. You know that you should act with compassion and do the right thing, but what does that mean in practice?

Time Out 25

What other examples of ethical codes do you know about? Which, if any, are followed in your class?

The Five Precepts

The 'yellow hat' song described the Five Precepts (maybe you could sing this song when you need to remember them), but it's not only Buddhist monks who will follow these precepts. Any Buddhist can follow them, and in so doing live according to the spirit (and the letter) of the Noble Eightfold Path. They aren't strict rules but training aids to help you make spiritual progress and live a harmonious life. They are usually expressed in a negative way, as a list of 'don'ts' or 'things to be avoided', as the following source shows.

The Five Precepts: the negative version

1 Do not take life

2 Do not take what is not given

3 Do not distort facts

4 Refrain from misuse of the senses

5 Refrain from self-intoxication through alcohol or drugs

Source: www.katinkahesselink.net/tibet/panchasila.html

Buddhism isn't a negative religion, full of prohibitions aiming to take the fun out of life (and as a teenager you know that the more someone tells you not to do something the more you want to do it). It is more useful to think of the Five Precepts more positively, because that's how they're meant to be. The Precepts are suggestions for practical ways in which you can put your Buddhist belief into action and so progress towards Nibbana. On the way, putting these into action will also help you show loving kindness and compassion. You don't know what your actions will lead to but that shouldn't stop you trying as hard as you can to live a compassionate life. Here the Five Precepts are expressed a little differently (and much more positively):

1   I will preserve life and cause no harm.

2   I will practise being generous and giving.

3   I will speak truthfully and listen carefully.

4   I will cultivate responsibility for the feelings of others.

5   I will expose my body only to healthy things.

Buddhists use the Precepts as guidance. They are not set in stone and they are always open to interpretation in line with the principle of skilful actions. And if you can't always manage to follow them all, you should at least try to follow some – it's a step in the right direction after all.

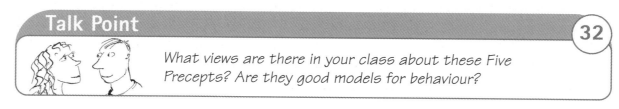

Talk Point   32

What views are there in your class about these Five Precepts? Are they good models for behaviour?

I will preserve life and cause no harm (Do not take life)

Are all Buddhists vegetarian? No. The Dalai Lama is said to have a little meat for lunch 'on doctor's orders' (though he does advocate vegetarianism). Buddhist monks who carry begging bowls into which lay people put their food are sometimes given meat and will eat it. In the high plateau of Tibet, being a vegetarian isn't terribly practical. Many Buddhists are vegetarian because of this very precept, but also many are not.

However, the principle remains that whenever possible, Buddhists should not take life or cause unnecessary harm. This is linked to the view that all living things participate in the cycle of Samsara and are struggling towards Enlightenment, so we should do all we can to help other living things along, not cut their journey short by taking their life or slowing their journey by causing them harm.

Many martial arts have Buddhist origins. In the past, Buddhist monks realised that they might have to defend themselves against attackers, but they did not want to kill or use weapons, so they developed forms of fighting back where the purpose was not to attack but defend. Often these were developed as hand-to-hand fighting practices. The aim wasn't to kill but to disarm the attacker using only the force that was necessary.

Buddhists should also refuse to support any action which causes harm or takes life. Being silent or inactive in response to the unnecessary taking of life is sometimes thought of being as just as bad as actually taking life. Buddhists are therefore often in the forefront of anti-war and anti-violence campaigns. In practice, the precept of preserving life means that Buddhists will show practical concern for all life. Buddhists will therefore encourage environmental protection and the preservation of species, as well as speaking out against any form of human rights abuse and working to end it. Taking life and even thinking aggressively have negative Kammic consequences for yourself and others, so you need to avoid doing this. If you go further and view all life as special then you won't even need to avoid the problem – for you it will never arise.

Talk Point 33

How might the principle of skilful actions affect the Precept of avoiding the taking of life?

I will practise being generous and giving (Do not take what is not given)

How many of the world's problems are caused by economic inequality? We often hear of people in undeveloped countries being paid only a pound or two per day for doing hard, dirty and dangerous work. Sometimes it's pretty startling that a few pounds really can save a life. How many times have you heard charities say things like, 'For just a few pounds a week you can …'? Buddhists believe that we should give when we can. It might be our money, our time or our expertise. It might just be being there for someone. It doesn't have to be grand to be a world-changing gesture.

Stealing something is obviously an example of taking what isn't given, and so is wrong. But the following example might be just as much 'stealing' as direct robbery:

15 year old Hannah shops at the 'KrazyKut Price Store' for her clothes. Things are incredibly cheap but don't look it, so Hannah buys lots of clothes (she gets loads of pocket money to spend). Hannah knows that the clothes are so cheap because they were made in a far-off land by people who are no more than slaves. Often these workers are just kids themselves. But Hannah just keeps on buying. After all, what can she do about it?

The Buddhist answer is pretty obvious: don't buy at KrazyKut any more. When we support this kind of exploitation we are effectively stealing. We are not rewarding the workers properly for their time – a form of theft – and therefore taking what has not been given. Giving people what they deserve for their efforts and not depriving them of what is rightfully theirs is loving kindness in action.

Time Out (26)

Is buying cheap goods made by poorly paid workers stealing?

Giving, not stealing

The giver who makes gifts to the lowliest poor of the city, considering them as worthy of offering as the Buddha himself, the giver who gives without any discrimination, impartially, with no expectation of reward, and with great love – this giver, I say, fulfils the perfection of giving.

Source: The Holy Teaching of Vimalakirti (trans.) R Thurman

I will speak truthfully and listen carefully (Do not distort facts/lie)

Have you heard the phrase 'being economical with the truth'? It doesn't mean outright lying as such. Instead, it usually means not giving all the facts and telling things in a particular way, usually in order to achieve a goal – so that the truth gets lost somewhere. We've probably all done this. But remember that skilful action means that well intentioned 'white lies' might sometimes be necessary and the right thing to do according to the situation, and that the rightness of such actions will depend on the motive behind them.

This Precept goes further than this, however. Lying because of greed, hatred or ignorance is obviously bad, but what about lying because you haven't really thought about what you are saying in the first place? Imagine the following scene: a teacher asks a pupil, 'Did you hear what I just said?' and the pupil replies, 'Yes', when the answer should have been 'No' (because the pupil's ears were blocked with mp3 player headphones). This is an unthinking response, and is an odd form of lie, but it is just as wrong as conscious lying ever is. The Zen Monk, Thich Nhat Hahn explains this Precept as meaning:

◆ don't tell outright lies

◆ don't exaggerate and claim something is what it is not

◆ don't say one thing to one person and a different thing to another

◆ don't say things to people that you don't mean (and don't say hurtful things that you do mean!).

Talk Point 34

When did you last exaggerate? What possible consequences could there have been?

How often do we have conversations with people when we're not listening very closely to what they are saying, but just waiting desperately for our next chance to say something? When we do this kind of thing we are actually 'lying' about listening to the person, because we're thinking about what we want to say and we're not listening at all. Also, when we gossip about people, we tend to mix fact with fiction – we exaggerate and maybe play one person off against another. And why do we gossip anyway? Not to build up the person we're gossiping about and show them loving kindness? No chance! Usually we do this either to knock the other person or to raise ourselves in the standing of the person we are gossiping with. In practice, therefore, this Precept is very closely linked to the principle of Right Speech, and using your words for good purposes.

I will cultivate responsibility for the feelings of others (Do not misuse the senses)

This Precept is sometimes thought to be only about sex. It's not. Although Buddhist monks and nuns abstain from sex, lay Buddhists don't have to. Nor do sexually active Buddhists have to be married. The ordained abstain from sex because sex can involve powerful emotions which can easily take control of you. It can lead you to being less mindful of what you are trying to do in life, that is,

THE MEANS

attain Nibbana. The power of the emotions associated with sex can lead to sex being the source of carelessness, thoughtlessness and disregard for others. If you

use someone for your own enjoyment, then you are not showing them respect (nor are you showing much self-respect). Sex can also be something destructive. It can be something you spend too much time thinking about and can divert your energies away from following the right paths of Buddhism. In itself sex isn't right or wrong in Buddhism, but it is something with the power to make you stray off the path to Enlightenment.

However, this Precept is also more generally about attachment. We live in a world where our senses are overloaded – there's so much information and so many ways of being entertained. For example, how many people with hundreds of cable TV channels will still complain that 'there's nothing on'? And what about that teenage mantra 'there's nothing to do round here'. Is that really true? When we look for constant stimulation of our senses (in whatever way, sexual or otherwise), we go against this precept. Using others for our enjoyment, even if that's just watching them on TV, could be considered a misuse of the senses. We become attached to the sensory pleasures of our world and they end up replacing what is real. We make a false reality which takes us away from understanding the true nature of Reality and reduces our chances of becoming one with it.

On women

The danger of women to monks was illustrated by some well-known advice said to have been given by the Buddha himself. His disciple Ananda asked: 'How are we to behave towards women?' The Buddha answered: 'Do not look at them'. Ananda objected: 'But if we have to see them, what shall we do?' The Buddha said: 'Do not talk to them'. Ananda persisted: 'But if they speak to us, what shall we do then?' The Buddha warned: 'Keep wide awake Ananda'.

Source: as quoted in 'Sexual Morality in the World's Religions' by G. Parrinder

Time Out 27

Can sex be abused?

I will expose my body only to healthy things (Refrain from self-intoxication through alcohol or drugs)

Not long ago a primary schoolgirl in Glasgow was discovered to have been smoking heroin for over two months. Everyone was horrified. But why? Is it worse for a primary school pupil to be addicted to drugs than anyone else? Buddhists believe that drugs (of any kind) are bad because of the effect they can have on self-control. Buddhism is all about mindfulness and developing awareness which leads to the practice of loving kindness. This is hard to achieve if you're out of your head, isn't it? Whether it's hard drugs or alcohol, the principle is the same – anything which clouds your mind and makes you less aware of reality isn't good. After all, people usually take drugs (and alcohol) to change their reality, or to hide from it. That would be the opposite of the Buddhist ideal (which is, of course, about finding Reality).

But this Precept covers more than just this. Drugs and alcohol don't just harm you, they can also harm others. Harm to others can be caused by accidents resulting from intoxication or by the violence which too often accompanies it. The whole drugs industry is pretty horrible. Drug selling and drug use is closely linked to all sorts of other crimes. If you take drugs, you fuel that whole nasty machine.

More than that though, Buddhists would say that you should think very carefully about the stuff you take into your body. You should avoid eating foods which have been produced without due care for nature, as well as foods which are exploitative – where the producer isn't paid fairly for his efforts. Eating should be done in moderation – enough to enjoy and sustain life. Overeating is sometimes a way of escaping from Reality into a false world of sensory pleasures. Foods should be wholesome and allow you to remain in control of yourself.

Living the right life means following these Precepts as closely as you can. From these Five Precepts, it is clear that Buddhists have high ethical standards. It is important to remember that this isn't because they're going to be 'judged'. It's because right or wrong thoughts, actions, words and so on all have Kammic consequences. *Doing* the right thing will lead to you *being* the right thing – cause and effect again – and help you move closer to your goals.

More morality for monks and nuns

In addition to the Five Precepts which all Buddhists should aim to keep, Buddhist monks and nuns have additional rules to follow.

I vow to abstain from taking untimely meals

This rule is linked to the Precept of exposing the body only to healthy things. You're far less likely (in theory) to overeat if you only eat at certain times of the day, or don't eat beyond a particular time. Also, monks and nuns generally are prohibited from cooking – again avoiding the temptation of

over-consumption. Apart from this, monks and nuns depend on the support of the lay community for their survival. In return they help the lay people in many ways, including teaching them and setting examples of how to make progress towards Nibbana. If you don't have to think about food (where it comes from, how it will be prepared, and so on) it's one less thing to get in the way of contemplation and practising loving kindness.

I vow to abstain from dancing, music, singing and watching mime

This rule covers virtually all forms of entertainment. It's not meant to be a killjoy approach to life; rather, it's another attempt to keep people who have become monks or nuns from straying from the path they have chosen. Looking to be entertained suggests that you want to create your own reality or hide from what is actually real by engaging in emotionally stimulating fantasy. To be a monk or nun you have agreed to seek the Truth. These entertainments are only likely to get in the way of that.

Time Out 28

How would your life change if you had to observe these two additional Precepts?

I vow to abstain from using perfumes and personal adornment

Odour free deodorant

May be suitable for monks and nuns

Apart from the fact that many perfumes are made in ethically questionable ways, the wearing of perfume suggests an attachment to the self – satisfaction of the senses and a desire for attention, or at least for people to think nicely of you. Wearing perfume suggests you have put yourself high up your list of priorities. Masking a human smell with the smell of something false is also quite an unreal act. Again, the perfumed person is creating a reality which is false and detracting from their true self. Oddly enough, perfumes were originally created to cover up the fact the people didn't wash very often and so were quite smelly. Monks and nuns take their own cleanliness very seriously, however; not using perfume today doesn't mean that you'll smell – it just means that you'll smell *real*. Adornments like jewellery and so on are prohibited for the same kinds of reason. They become sensual in themselves, suggesting the wearer has a selfish nature rather than a selfless one.

I vow to abstain from the use of high seats

This sound a bit bizarre, but it is just a vow that relates to comfort. The monk or nun shouldn't be uncomfortable (that would be extreme, with the likely outcome that the discomfort would be distracting), but nor should he or she be so comfortable that they get carried away with pleasure. A seat which is not too luxurious is the ideal. In practice, many monks and nuns get up very early and meditate; a combination of sleepiness and comfort might encourage them to nod off and so lose the benefit of their meditation and move away from

Enlightenment instead of towards it. In some monasteries, monks who do fall asleep are rather abruptly awakened with a thwack from a large stick. So a less comfortable seat has its advantages! The Buddha rejected both extreme pleasure and extreme asceticism. 'High seats' is just an example of this – if you are either too uncomfortable or too comfortable, your mind won't be on the right path.

Talk Point (35)

Do life's little luxuries sometimes keep you from doing things that you should?

I vow to abstain from handling money

So that's why robes haven't got pockets

In most monastic communities, lay people help by dealing with the day-to-day business affairs – paying the window cleaner and the like. The world's religions are united in their concerns about the fact that money can have a corrupting effect. Most religions have had teachers or leaders whose fondness for taking money has contaminated them. To avoid the potential pitfalls associated with taking and using money, monks and nuns just have nothing to do with it. This helps them avoid all the many temptations that

money can bring with it. It also helps them to do what they do without thinking of the possibility of any material reward.

The Five Precepts help all Buddhists to live a good life, and these extra vows help the ordained monks and nuns lead 'better' lives in the stricter sense. They help them to concentrate on what really matters, helping them avoid the more negative aspects of life and not become too attached to the more positive ones.

A monk's life

In the daily lives of monks and nuns there is wide variety of practice depending upon the tradition or school of Buddhism to which the monk or nun belongs. Many in monastic communities spend a great deal of time meditating, either in groups or individually. At Samye Ling in Dumfriesshire there is a retreat away from the temple which monks and nuns can go to for several years of solitude and reflection. Other monks engage in social activities which are aimed at helping people. This might be by teaching them about Buddhism, or it might be practical activities designed to help people in need. Tim Ward, a Canadian, spent time at a Theravada jungle monastery in Thailand called Wat Pah Nanachat, run by the Abbot, Ajahn Chah. This is a place where those from the West can not only learn about Buddhism but experience it too. Tim describes a typical day in the following source.

The daily routine

I wandered back into the empty sala [*temple*] and noticed a blackboard on the back wall. The daily schedule was written out in English.

3:00am – Rise

3:30am – Morning chanting, daily reflection and meditation

5:00am – Clean sala

Dawn – alms round [*this is a tradition in Thai Theravada Buddhism which involves going round with begging bowls for food; the monk cannot ask for food, but the local lay people provide it and believe that it is a source of good Kamma for them*]

8:00am – Meal

2:30pm – Drink

3:00pm – Chores

Lots of time, it appeared, to sit and watch the body breathe. Or walk back and forth among the scorpions.

Source: What the Buddha Never Taught, by Tim Ward (text in italics is author's explanation)

Much of Tim's time otherwise was taken up with listening to talks from the Abbot and carrying out basic maintenance of the temple mindfully. In Thailand it is not uncommon to have a skeleton in the temple to remind people of the impermanence of life. Tim also tells of a woman who had visited the temple over many years. A year after she died her husband agreed to have her body exhumed. A monk who had become her friend agreed to prepare her skeleton for display. So every day he went out to the jungle and slowly removed the flesh using his food knife. He did this as a meditation on death.

Not all monks do such peculiar things, but generally speaking the monastic life is study, meditation and activities which are designed to help you reflect on the Dhamma. Other monks and nuns are engaged in more direct social action: Thich Nhat Hahn, the Vietnamese Zen monk, thought by many to be a living Bodhisattva, describes how Buddhist temples helped children during the Vietnam War. He talks about street children who call themselves 'the dust of life', who are homeless and survive by eating what they find on garbage heaps. The monks and nuns in Ho Chi Minh City opened the temples to these children, taught them to read and write, fed them and played with them. He reported that the cost of feeding the children two meals a day was only twenty cents (of course, the time spent with the children was free), and then he adds:

Generosity

It takes time to help these children, not much money. There are so many simple things like this that we can do to help people, but because we cannot free ourselves from our situation and our lifestyle, we do nothing at all.

Source: dharma.ncf.ca/introduction/precepts/precept-2.html

Finally, you should remember that in Theravada Buddhism the ideal is the Arhat and in Mahayana it is the Bodhisattva (see pages 84–87). These beings would have accepted and lived according to all the Precepts above and many more besides. Remember that these Enlightened beings have already attained Nibbana. In practice, this means that their lives would be lived according to the highest moral standards.

THE MEANS

Activities

Knowledge, Understanding, Evaluation

1 Why should Buddhists do good?

2 Do you think rules are better described as 'don'ts' or 'dos'? Explain.

3 Who should follow the Five Precepts?

4 Should Buddhists be vegetarian?

5 How might kung fu demonstrate the First Precept?

6 In what ways can Buddhists put the First Precept into action?

7 How might a Buddhist define stealing?

8 How does Vimalakirti describe perfect giving?

9 Why might a Buddhist think that exaggerating goes against the Third Precept?

10 What's wrong with gossip?

11 What do you think the Buddha meant by advising his disciple Ananda to keep wide awake?

12 Why is sex something the Buddhist should be careful about?

13 In what ways might TV watching go against the Fourth Precept?

14 Why do you think many lay Buddhists don't drink and monks and nuns are not allowed to?

15 How is alcohol linked to mindfulness?

16 In what ways is Buddhist morality all to do with consequences?

17 Why might it be easier for monks and nuns to follow more precepts and rules than lay people?

18 Why should monks and nuns not take 'untimely meals'?

19 Why would you be unlikely to find at monk at the cinema?

20 Is it better to smell real than to wear perfume?

21 Buddhist monks and nuns usually sleep on mats or hard beds. Why do you think this is?

22 In a Buddhist temple, who might pay the window cleaner and why?

23 Do you think any of the five precepts is more important than the others? Explain your answer.

24 What does Tim Ward say his day is mostly about?

25 How did the monks and nuns of Ho Chi Minh City put loving kindness into action?

26 What moral standards would Arhats and Bodhisattvas follow?

Practical Activities

1 Make up an information leaflet for people your age showing them how they could put the five precepts into action in their lives. Make sure that you link it very closely to the likely lifestyle of someone your age. What kinds of things will they no longer be allowed to do? What should they be doing instead? Also, why should they be doing it. . .?

2 Do your own version of the 'yellow hat' song covering the additional Precepts for monks and nuns.

3 Imagine a Scottish man, interested in becoming a Buddhist monk, goes to a monastery to ask about what it will involve. Script the conversation (with some humour) between him and the head monk he speaks to.

4 Find examples of moral stories from newspapers and magazines. For each one, use your understanding of Buddhist ethics to discuss how a Buddhist might respond to the issues.

Unit Assessment Question

Int 1 'I will abstain from taking what is not given.' Explain TWO different Buddhist understandings of this Precept. *(4)*

Int 2 What is meant by the Precept 'Do not distort facts'? *(2)*

Higher

What different understandings might Buddhists have about the Precept against the taking of life? *(8)*

Sample Exam Question

Int 1 State one Precept which only monks and nuns are expected to observe. *(1KU)*

Int 2 'The Precept "Refrain from the misuse of the senses" is only about sexual morality.' Would a Buddhist agree? Give reasons for your answer. *(2KU, 2AE)*

Higher

Explain why a Buddhist monk or nun should avoid high chairs. *(2KU, 2AE)*

Homework

Watch a news item on TV which covers an issue of morality. Report what the item is about, and explain how a Buddhist might respond to it based on your understanding of the five precepts.

Personal Reflection

Could you follow the Five Precepts? How might your life improve if you did? (Would it?)

Meditation and Worship

*In the book, **Buddha Da**, Anne Donovan tells the tale of an ordinary Glasgow man who becomes a Buddhist, while his daughter Anne Marie finds it all very strange...*

MA DA's a nutter. Radio rental. He'd dae anything for a laugh so he wid; went doon the shops wi a perra knickers on his heid, tellt the wifie next door we'd won the lottery and were flittin tae Barbados, but that wis daft stuff compared tae whit he's went an done noo. He's turnt intae a Buddhist.

[...] he'd startit meditatin in the hoose every night for aboot hauf an hour. Ah decided tae ask him aboot it.

'Da?'

'Aye hen.'

'See this meditation, whit is it?'

He pulled a face.

'Ah'm no sure how tae stert. It's difficult tae explain.'

'Aye, but whit d'you dae?'

'Well you sit doon quiet and you try tae empty yer mind, well no exactly empty, mair quiet it doon so aw the thoughts that go fleein aboot in yer heid kinda slow doon and don't annoy ye.'

'Why?'

'Ah'm no very sure masel, hen.'

'D'you like daein it?'

He smiled. 'Aye hen, ah dae.'

'Mibbe that's why.'

'Mibbe you're right. That's dead profound. Mibbe you're a Buddhist and you don't know it.'

'Ah don't think ah want tae be a Buddhist, Daddy.'

'How no, hen?'

'If ah went tae meditate wi you ah'd miss *Who Wants to Be a Millionaire*.'

Source: Buddha Da, by Anne Donovan

What is and is not meditation

Meditation is probably one of the first things which come to mind when people think about Buddhism. People often wrongly assume (like Donnie did about Rab, see pages 27–29) that it's about sitting around not doing anything and contemplating your navel. This is not the case. Although it is central to Buddhism, meditation is not an end in itself – it is just one of the many means helping you on your travels towards ultimate Enlightenment. Even the Enlightened continue to meditate, so it must have functions in addition to attaining Nibbana. (However, that does raise the interesting question of what the Enlightened being does after attaining Enlightenment. . .)

Westerners often dip into meditation despite not adhering to any other Buddhist ideas or practices. This may be personally beneficial, but it's not the same thing as fitting Buddhist meditation into a whole way of looking at and trying to experience reality. According to the Buddhist hermit Mr Chen, there are some common mistakes Buddhists and non-Buddhists make when meditating:

◆ they do not base their meditation on the foundations of renunciation; it is difficult to engage properly in meditation if you are still firmly attached to the things of this world

◆ they do not link their meditation to the practice of loving kindness in other aspects of their lives

◆ they use meditation for health benefits, like relaxation, not for spiritual purposes

◆ they think that meditation is only about the mind and not the body too

◆ they mix up all kinds of meditation from across religions

◆ they are not aware of the real function of meditation.

Source: based on an interview with Mr Chen at www.yogichen.org

 **Talk Point** 36

Have you ever tried meditation or any kind of relaxation technique?

It's obvious that meditation is important for Buddhists – after all, the Buddha attained Nibbana while meditating – so what is it? Most Buddhists agree that it is a stilling of the mind and an altered state of consciousness where the meditator can begin to perceive Reality differently. It's done actively, and so it's the opposite of unconscious thinking (which is passive 'tuning out'). While meditating you should be ultra conscious and aware of things as they really are. In daily life, the mind is continually active and strays around subjects almost constantly. One of the functions of meditation is to train it not to do so and to focus completely on specifics. Once you have achieved this state of mind, or rather being (and there are numerous levels of achieving this), you will be in a

THE MEANS

far better position to realise the true meaning of many of the Buddhist ideas that this book has covered. For most Buddhists, learning the theory, as you have been doing, is not enough – you have to practise and experience it too. To truly understand meditation you need to do it. Rab had the right idea after all.

There are many varieties of meditation practised by the different schools of Buddhism throughout the world. Cultural influences might slightly alter the forms of meditation you find in different regions. Depending on where you are, meditation might be done sitting, standing, walking or in the traditional cross-legged lotus position. Some Buddhists are completely silent during meditation while others chant mantras or passages of scripture. You can meditate by focusing on an image of the Buddha, whether it's a very plain one or something more ornate like a Thangka (see pages 96–97), or you can meditate using ornate patterns like mandalas. Alternatively, you can meditate on the teachings of the Buddha, either generally like the Three Jewels or more specifically on passages from Buddhist scriptures.

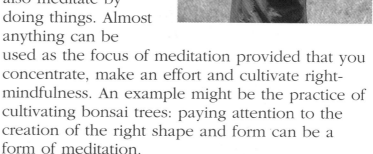

You can also sit and meditate on everyday objects, for example, a flower or a tree. You can even meditate on the fact of your breathing in and out or walking one foot in front of the other. You can also meditate by doing things. Almost anything can be used as the focus of meditation provided that you concentrate, make an effort and cultivate right-mindfulness. An example might be the practice of cultivating bonsai trees: paying attention to the creation of the right shape and form can be a form of meditation.

The Buddha taught that there are seven benefits of meditation:

◆ getting rid of defilements

◆ putting aside sorrow and worry

- getting over miseries
- ending physical suffering
- ending mental suffering
- attaining the early stages of Nibbana
- attaining Nibbana itself.

All forms of meditation have the same thing in common: mindfulness of the things around you, that is, seeing things as they really are. There are, however, two main types of meditation (and a specific version of these in Zen Buddhism): stilling and revealing.

Time Out (29)

Close your eyes for three minutes. How easy is it to think of nothing?

Samatha meditation: Stilling

Calming the mind

By regular daily practice, the chattering unruly mind gradually becomes calmer and clearer. The way our mind works becomes less confusing to us and we begin to understand the habits of mind that hold us back from happiness and freedom. We become kinder to ourselves and those around us. Meditation is a practical matter: increased peace and awareness bring an ability to make the most of ourselves in our daily lives.

Source: www.samatha.org/meditation/index.html

This kind of meditation is sometimes referred to as 'calming meditation' and is linked most closely to the Theravada tradition. The aim of this kind of meditation is to still or calm the mind. Increasingly we are bombarded with images and ideas – advertising messages are everywhere, there are hundreds of TV and radio channels, DVDs, CDs, magazines, newspapers, books, computers, mobile phones. It is difficult for people's minds to be at rest. When they are not at rest, 'fleein aboot', it is difficult to think about what really matters. Samatha meditation aims to calm and still the mind so that you are not distracted by the millions of things which constantly surround you. This is the first step in being more able to see things as they really are and beginning to develop a more mindful approach to life generally.

When you are mindful (that is, thinking consciously about what you are doing), you are more likely to be able to engage in understanding the teachings of the Buddha, and put them into practice for the benefit of yourself and everyone else.

 THE MEANS

Stillness therefore is the first step of meditation (and so, eventually Enlightenment). When you start Samatha meditation you may just concentrate on the act of breathing. Thoughts will come into your head, and as they do, you should simply be aware of them and let them pass. If you try too hard to push them away you'll end up concentrating on them instead of your breathing.

> ## Talk Point
>
> *Try it: whatever you do right now, do NOT get a picture in your mind of a pineapple. Why was it difficult not to think of a pineapple?*

This kind of meditation is said to have levels of trance. (You need to be aware that, in translating some of the original words into English, some of the 'bigger picture' aspects of meditation are lost, so your idea of a 'trance' might be something quite different.) These levels of trance are called Jhana. The lowest level could be called 'Jhana lite', which is thought of as where your mind becomes detached and full of joy, and the highest level is the eighth Jhana, which involves neither perception nor non-perception. The only way to understand what this means is to experience it for yourself. For any of these states to be achieved you have to completely banish ill-will, sensual thought, laziness, restlessness, worry and doubting. Many Buddhists believe that at some of the higher Jhana stages you achieve psychic powers like mind-reading and clairvoyance. It would obviously be completely wrong and contrary to Buddhist teaching to meditate only so that you could gain such powers, because this would be using meditation so satisfy some pretty dubious desires.

All of this is rather complicated, so many Buddhists suggest that a more practical approach is to meditate using the following four ideas:

◆ meditating by thinking positive thoughts about all beings – starting with self-love and radiating out love to all (Metta)

◆ meditating on how you can help others who suffer (Karuna)

◆ sharing the joy of others who are happy (Mudita)

◆ experiencing love for everything equally (Upekkha).

Vipassana meditation: Revealing

This is sometimes referred to as 'insight meditation'. This is more focused concentration on the true reality of things, leading to a proper insight into the way things are. This is where, as well as learning the theories, you also experience what they mean, so giving you insight into what they are really about. As with all forms of meditation, newcomers are encouraged to find an experienced person to teach them meditation (rather than trying to learn it from books), because it alters your way of thinking about things, making you think about things in unusual ways. Vipassana meditation gradually strips away the layers of experience in life, revealing things for what they are. This could be quite scary (and weird) if you're not fully prepared for it and supported by a teacher. For example, you probably think of your body as just the outer you. You probably don't imagine what you would look like if your body were peeled layer by layer – what might your skeleton look like, for example? Or your heart? Vipassana encourages this kind of deep reflection and so concentrates on the links between mind and body and the interconnectedness of all things. This leads to awareness of the true nature of Reality which is so often disguised by rational and logical thinking.

Vipassana meditation

[Vipassana meditation] may correctly be applied to any Buddhist meditation technique that aims for a complete understanding of the Three Characteristics – dukkha, anicca and anatta.

Source: www.vipassana.com

Time Out ⟨30⟩

Do this with teacher supervision. Sit comfortably and think about something like a car. Gradually remove each part of the car, piece by piece. Are you thinking any differently about the car?

Some Buddhists, but not all, believe that Samatha meditation is something you do before you can move on to Vipassana meditation.

Samatha and Vipassana meditation

Although Buddhism sees many benefits in *samatha* meditation, it is not said to ultimately lead to enlightenment. Although calm, equanimity and bliss are attained, the condition is only temporary. True realisation requires the insight into the nature of reality that *vipassana* meditation offers.

Source: www.heartwood2000.com/Samatha.html

THE MEANS

Zen meditation: Quizzing

Zen meditation (known as Ch'an in China) goes one step beyond Samatha and Vipassana meditation. It stresses the experience side of what meditation can bring you. It's said that the Buddha once held a flower in his hand and turned it round – thus teaching the Dhamma. If this makes no sense then that's the point (inasmuch as there is a point). Zen uses art, poetry and spontaneous outbursts to try to achieve insight leading to Enlightenment. Zen Buddhists believe that only an Enlightened being can lead you to Enlightenment so he helps you with the practice of meditation. One well known way of doing this is the koan. These are nonsensical quizzes or statements which can't be grasped in any logical way, but then, should they even be grasped? (You would have to ask an Enlightened being about that.) Probably the most well known koan is, 'What is the sound of one hand clapping?' But a koan can also take the form of a question and nonsensical answer, for example:

Question: Why have you taken RMPS this year?
Answer: Custard is best cold.

A koan like this uses the idea that even the meaning of words is impermanent, thus reinforcing the concept of impermanence generally and perhaps moving the person a step closer to understanding.

Zazen meditation is also a bit different to the other two because it involves sitting – just sitting. The founder of Zen, Bodhidharma, is said to have spent nine years sitting staring at a wall. Zen meditation may seem very weird to you, but maybe that's the point – maybe everything just is weird. Maybe once you understand that you're Enlightened (then again, maybe not).

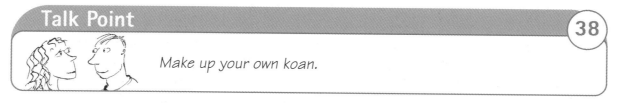

Talk Point

(38)

Make up your own koan.

Whatever the form of meditation, the purpose is the same. You cannot *learn* to be a Buddhist – you have to *experience* it for yourself. Even the simplest parts of Buddhist teaching make more sense if you experience them in your being rather than just hold them in your head as stored information. Meditation is the way to do this.

Godless worship?

Many non-Buddhists don't understand Buddhist worship (Puja), wondering what Buddhists could worship when they don't believe in a God. The simplest explanation might be that many Buddhists do believe in gods and in helpful and unhelpful supernatural beings. Worship helps you stay on the right side of the helpful ones and keeps the unhelpful ones at a distance. Mahayana Buddhists also believe that appealing to Bodhisattvas has some Kammic merit and can be helpful in your progression towards Enlightenment.

It is important to understand what is meant by 'worship'. Worship has different dimensions and elements in all religions, and it is no different in Buddhism. During worship you can honour the Buddha and show him reverence, learn from his teachings and share with others in your common journey of life. You can gain spiritual support from people and you can give it too. Worship gives your faith structure and expression, and the communal element can provide benefits that are otherwise unavailable if you practise your faith on your own. Worship can also allow you to give very abstract ideas a concrete form. You can use symbols to represent teachings and beliefs – you can take complex concepts and make them visual. All of this can help you make progress and so it is all an example of skilful actions. However, the Buddha warned against being too attached to ceremonies and rituals, teaching that these should not replace following the Eightfold Paths.

Buddhist worship can also involve the recitation of key Buddhist ideas like taking refuge in the Three Jewels and accepting the Five Precepts. Worship can also be occasions for important teachers to pass on their understanding of the Dhamma or to lead worshippers in meditation of one kind or another.

Attitudes to worship differ slightly between the Theravada and Mahayana schools of Buddhism.

Theravada worship

For monks and nuns, worship is rarely more than reciting Buddhist teachings and meditating. Lay Buddhists will do this too, but may also make offerings to Buddha statues, pray to the Buddha, and carry out a wide variety of religious practices which are more likely to have their origins in the religion which existed in that land before Buddhism arrived than in the Dhamma. Such as it is, Theravada worship is very simplistic and focuses very much on the image of Buddha. Other aspects of religious practices can also be considered as acts of reverence, for example, the provision of food for the monastic community by lay people. For Theravadins, much of this can be thought of as resulting in building up good Kamma for a better rebirth (hopefully as a monk or nun), but it is also a simple way of sharing the theory and practice of Buddhism.

THE MEANS

Mahayana worship

This is generally much more elaborate, colourful and varied. Mahayana worship includes chanting, special rituals for certain events or times of year, mantras chanted or written on fluttering prayer-flags and so on. You can spin prayer wheels which contain mantras, and these throw off good thoughts as they spin. (You can even install something on your computer so that as your hard drive spins around it acts as a prayer wheel.) In Tibet, prayer wheels can be hand-held and used while you walk or they can be huge permanent arrangements, spun as you pass them in the street. In Mahayana Buddhism, prayers are often made to Bodhisattvas in the hope that they can help you with your life and your spiritual progress. It is sometimes difficult to know, however, when a particular aspect of Mahayana worship relates directly to the teachings of the Buddha and when it derives from local folklore and popular religion.

Buddhist shrines

Buddhist shrines vary greatly according to the form of Buddhism. In Mahayana temples, there will probably be a great number of images or statues of the Buddha, as well as statues and images of Bodhisattvas. There might also be pictures of people who are important to a particular branch of Buddhism, such as the Dalai Lama or other lamas in Tibetan Buddhism. Texts may be placed in cabinets as much for reverence as for reading. There will probably be gongs, bells, incense, drums and all manner of devices for making sounds. Prayer flags may flutter from the ceiling, and there may be all sorts of other objects, for example, 'holy relics' of special people in that tradition. There could be mandalas and other symbolic items around the shrine-room. (Before Samye Ling in Dumfriesshire was a great temple, the local Buddhist community worshipped in a converted house. There was a home-made prayer wheel made from an old-fashioned record covered with mantras spinning around on a record player!) There may also be lots of symbols, some more closely linked to 'magic' and superstition than to what you now understand as Buddhism.

By contrast, although Zen is a form of Mahayana Buddhism, a Zen shrine will be as simple as possible – it can even be a raked garden of sand. It may contain no

images at all – nothing to distract you from the practice of meditation.

Theravada shrines will be centred on an image or a statue of the Buddha in one of the forms discussed in section 7 (see pages 92–97). Out of reverence for the image, flowers and offerings may be made. The image itself will help 'worshippers' because it will

probably have symbols which remind them of essential Buddhist ideas. Again though, the shrine may reflect local customs more than the actual tradition of Buddhism. Tim Ward, the Canadian who spent time in the Theravadin vihara Wat Pah Nanachat in Thailand, reports that, as well as very ornate Buddha images, the shrine room also contained:

◆ the skeleton of the mother of a girl who still visited the shrine (see page 139 for this gruesome story)

◆ a dead human baby in a large jar of preserving fluid

◆ the photograph of a man who was found dead and well-preserved in a cave; he was naked and sitting in the lotus position apparently having died while meditating.

Talk Point 39

Both the skeleton and the dead baby remind us of the impermanence of life. What purpose do you think the photograph serves?

Again, Buddhist shrines show a great deal of variety according to their tradition. But all have in common the idea of helping people with the practice of removing ignorance and replacing it with understanding, based on the teachings of the Buddha. This can be a source of spiritual nourishment which helps the worshipper to put loving kindness into action and to live compassionately. Skilful actions allows for all sorts of variation here – if an action helps the individual make progress towards Nibbana, then it's good.

Activities

Knowledge, Understanding, Evaluation

1 What is meditation not?

2 Explain one mistake people often make about meditation according to Mr Chen.

3 What fact about the Buddha's life suggests that meditation is important?

4 Describe one way of meditating.

5 What are the benefits of meditation for Buddhists?

6 According to the source on page 145, what is Samatha meditation for?

7 Why might Samatha meditation be particularly important in the 21st century?

8 How does meditation help you to be mindful?

9 Why should a Buddhist not try to develop the psychic powers that might arise from meditation?

10 Give an example from your own experience of a time when you have demonstrated insight.

11 Why should you do Vipassana meditation only with an experienced guide?

12 According to the source on page 147, in what way is Samatha meditation not enough?

13 How does Zen help you to progress towards Enlightenment?

14 What is the purpose of a koan?

15 How would you answer the koan about the hand clapping?

16 What is the purpose of meditation for Buddhists?

17 Describe one thing a Buddhist would do during worship?

18 What do Buddhists worship?

19 Why do Buddhists worship?

20 What might a Theravadin lay person think was one of the benefits of Puja?

21 Describe two similarities and two differences between worship in the Theravada and Mahayana traditions.

22 What is the purpose of a prayer wheel?

23 How does where Buddhists live affect the kind of worship they do?

24 Describe a typical Theravada shrine.

25 Choose two objects in a Mahayana shrine and explain their purpose.

26 Do you think objects help or distract Buddhists from practising Buddhism?

27 How do meditation and worship help Buddhists to make progress towards Enlightenment?

Practical Activities

1 Imagine Anne Marie went along to her Da's Buddhist centre. She agreed to try out some basic meditation with her Da. It was Theravadin. Describe, in the same style as the stimulus if you can, what she would see and experience there.

2 Make up an information leaflet – Buddhist meditation: Facts and Fiction.

3 Make your own Buddha image as a focus for a display in your classroom. After making it you could set it up as a shrine in either a Theravada or Mahayana style (be respectful in doing so).

4 Try some real meditation. With your teacher's approval, invite a practising Buddhist to do this with you.

5 Use the four ideas – Metta, Karuna, Mudita and Upekkha – as the basis for either written text for a meditation or images and ideas which could be used as a focus for meditation.

6 Make up a few koans. Pass them round and see what answers people come up with.

7 Make your own version of one of the objects associated with Buddhist worship.

Unit Assessment Question

Int 1 Describe a typical Mahayana Buddhist shrine.   *(6)*

Int 2 Describe TWO differences between Theravada and Mahayana worship.   *(4)*

Higher

'In the 21st century, Samatha meditation is needed more than ever.' Would Buddhists agree?   *(8)*

Sample Exam Question

Int 1 Describe how a Buddhist might carry out Vipassana meditation.   *(4KU)*

Int 2 What is the purpose of Samatha meditation?   *(4KU)*

Higher

'Meditation helps you progress towards Nibbana.' How would a Buddhist support this statement?   *(4KU, 4AE)*

Homework

Find out about and write a short report about the Japanese tea ceremony. In what way is this considered to be meditation?

Personal Reflection

What could meditation do for you?

Textual Sources

Dhammapada 76–82, 89

Dhammapada text	Commentary
76 If you see an intelligent man who tells you where true treasures are to be found, who shows what is to be avoided, and administers reproofs, follow that wise man; it will be better, not worse, for those who follow him.	*No one likes to be told that they're wrong or that their behaviour is poor. But sometimes we need to be told this to open our eyes to how we are. Instead of being defensive about it we should welcome such honesty and learn from it – treat it as helpful as opposed to nit-picking.*
77 Let him admonish, let him teach, let him forbid what is improper! – he will be beloved of the good, by the bad he will be hated.	*Perhaps today people (and maybe young people especially) aren't told often enough that some things are wrong and some are right. Personal freedom is one thing but that shouldn't mean that we just accept everything or do what we like. Morality matters! And remember, a row can be constructive too.*
78 Do not have evil-doers for friends, do not have low people for friends: have virtuous people for friends, have for friends the best of men.	*If you associate with bad people don't be surprised if their badness rubs off on you. Seek out people who'll build you up not knock you down and who will help you to be good rather than encourage you to be bad. This could be taken as justification for Buddhists living the monastic life or even just associating with other Buddhists.*
79 He who drinks in the law lives happily with a serene mind: the sage rejoices always in the dhamma, as preached by the elect (Ariyas).	*Principles for living a good life are a form of nourishment. If you take in what's right you'll act right. Listen to the wise and develop your own wisdom.*
80 Well-makers lead the water (wherever they like); fletchers bend the arrow; carpenters bend a log of wood; wise people fashion themselves.	*When you make something make sure that it's fit for the job. Are you fit for the job of progressing towards and attaining Enlightenment? If not, change the way you behave and make yourself spiritually and morally fit.*

81 As a solid rock is not shaken by the wind, wise people falter not amidst blame and praise.	*Observing good moral principles in your everyday life will enable you to weather the troubles life throws at you and remain solid in your determination to throw off the chains of ignorance.*
82 Wise people, after they have listened to the dhamma, become serene, like a deep, smooth, and still lake.	*How you should behave in life is sometimes very difficult to work out. Deciding what's right and what's wrong can throw you into turbulent confusion. Follow the Dhamma and this confusion will settle and be still.*
89 Those whose mind is well grounded in the (seven) elements of knowledge, who without clinging to anything, rejoice in freedom from attachment, whose appetites have been conquered, and who are full of light, are free (even) in this world.	*Enlightenment can only come when you are free from the attachments of this world. Many of these are very closely linked to our moral behaviour. So we have to act right before we can attain release from samsara. Remember that wrong action ties us to rebirth and right action frees us from it.*

Dhammapada 273–289

Dhammapada text	Commentary
273 The best of ways is the eightfold; the best of truths the four words; the best of virtues passionlessness; the best of men he who has eyes to see.	*The Noble Eightfold Path, the last of the Four Noble Truths, can open your eyes and free you from stumbling around in the darkness which is no way to Nibbana. The ignorant are blind to reality.*
274 This is the way, there is no other that leads to the purifying of intelligence. Go on this way! Everything else is the deceit of Mara.	*Mara will try to tempt you off the true path – resist! The Eightfold Path gives you the security of knowing how you should live a good life.*
275 If you go on this way, you will make an end of pain! The way was preached by me, when I had understood the removal of the thorns (in the flesh).	*The Buddha realised that suffering was a central feature to life and that it was caused by desire. To end its pain you have to live a life which isn't full of desire. The Eightfold Path shows you how to do this.*
276 You yourself must make an effort. The Buddhas are only preachers. The thoughtful who enter the way are freed from the bondage of Mara.	*You have to do this for yourself. You can learn it all in your head, but unless you put it into practice for yourself, you'll never really understand it. Use the Buddha's teaching as a starting-point.*
277 'All created things perish,' he who knows and sees this becomes passive in pain; this is the way to purity.	*Realising the fact of impermanence is the first step.*

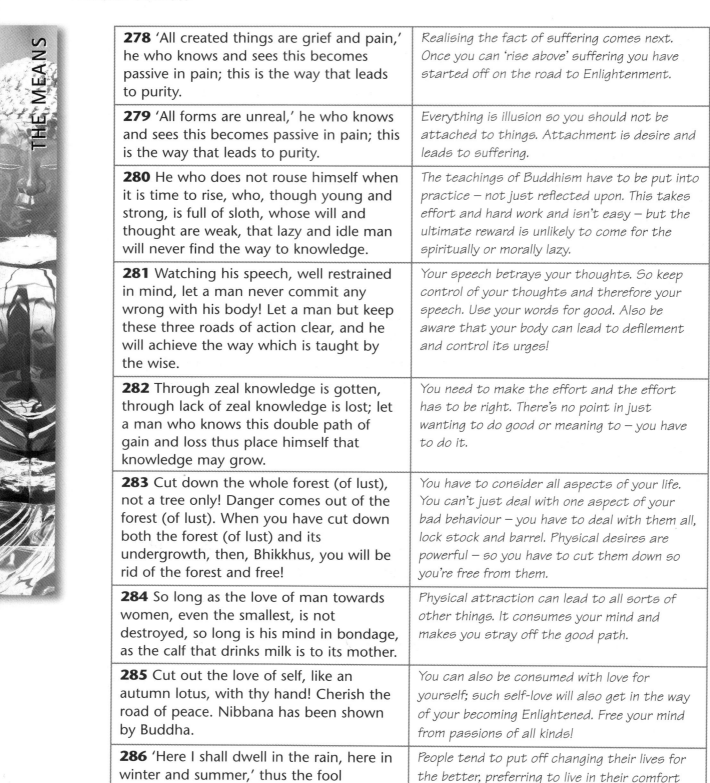

THE MEANS

278 'All created things are grief and pain,' he who knows and sees this becomes passive in pain; this is the way that leads to purity.	*Realising the fact of suffering comes next. Once you can 'rise above' suffering you have started off on the road to Enlightenment.*
279 'All forms are unreal,' he who knows and sees this becomes passive in pain; this is the way that leads to purity.	*Everything is illusion so you should not be attached to things. Attachment is desire and leads to suffering.*
280 He who does not rouse himself when it is time to rise, who, though young and strong, is full of sloth, whose will and thought are weak, that lazy and idle man will never find the way to knowledge.	*The teachings of Buddhism have to be put into practice – not just reflected upon. This takes effort and hard work and isn't easy – but the ultimate reward is unlikely to come for the spiritually or morally lazy.*
281 Watching his speech, well restrained in mind, let a man never commit any wrong with his body! Let a man but keep these three roads of action clear, and he will achieve the way which is taught by the wise.	*Your speech betrays your thoughts. So keep control of your thoughts and therefore your speech. Use your words for good. Also be aware that your body can lead to defilement and control its urges!*
282 Through zeal knowledge is gotten, through lack of zeal knowledge is lost; let a man who knows this double path of gain and loss thus place himself that knowledge may grow.	*You need to make the effort and the effort has to be right. There's no point in just wanting to do good or meaning to – you have to do it.*
283 Cut down the whole forest (of lust), not a tree only! Danger comes out of the forest (of lust). When you have cut down both the forest (of lust) and its undergrowth, then, Bhikkhus, you will be rid of the forest and free!	*You have to consider all aspects of your life. You can't just deal with one aspect of your bad behaviour – you have to deal with them all, lock stock and barrel. Physical desires are powerful – so you have to cut them down so you're free from them.*
284 So long as the love of man towards women, even the smallest, is not destroyed, so long is his mind in bondage, as the calf that drinks milk is to its mother.	*Physical attraction can lead to all sorts of other things. It consumes your mind and makes you stray off the good path.*
285 Cut out the love of self, like an autumn lotus, with thy hand! Cherish the road of peace. Nibbana has been shown by Buddha.	*You can also be consumed with love for yourself; such self-love will also get in the way of your becoming Enlightened. Free your mind from passions of all kinds!*
286 'Here I shall dwell in the rain, here in winter and summer,' thus the fool meditates, and does not think of his death.	*People tend to put off changing their lives for the better, preferring to live in their comfort zone. But you can't fool yourself forever – your beliefs and actions have consequences and they'll catch up with you.*

287 Death comes and carries off that man, praised for his children and flocks, his mind distracted, as a flood carries off a sleeping village.	*Thinking only of yourself you are creating the Kammic patterns for your continual rebirths. You will not make any spiritual progress unless you challenge yourself to live a better life.*
288 Sons are no help, nor a father, nor relations; there is no help from kinsfolk for one whom death has seized.	*Nothing will save you from the inevitable consequences of not following the suggestions of the Eightfold Path.*
289 A wise and good man who knows the meaning of this, should quickly clear the way that leads to Nirvana.	*The Eightfold Path helps you to cut your way through the strangling jungles of life and make your way clear for the journey towards Enlightenment.*

Textual work

The following is the kind of exam question you may meet in your RMPS exam. **Remember**, there are no prescribed sources at **Intermediate 1**.

Read the following source, then answer all of the parts of the question (a)–(e). The number of marks available for each part is indicated; use them to help you answer the question.

Dhammapada 81

'As a solid rock is not shaken by the wind, wise people falter not amidst blame and praise.'

(a) How can people 'falter' in life?   *(2KU)*

(b) Why might a Buddhist think that both blame and praise are to be avoided?   *(4AE)*

(c) Explain two elements of the Noble Eightfold Path.   *(6KU)*

(d) Choose one of the Five Precepts. Explain **how** and **why** a Buddhist might observe this Precept.   *(4KU, 4AE)*

(e) 'The Noble Eightfold Path, the Five Precepts and all the many rules for monks and nuns all come down to one basic thing: compassion.' Would a Buddhist agree?   *(5AE)*

(25 marks)

Revision and Study Guide

What's this course been for?

This has not been a course intended to turn you into a Buddhist. But you can if you want, wearing orange robes and meditating in the school dining hall – it's your choice. In studying this course you will have had a chance to explore a bit more what you think about the beliefs and practices you've studied. Maybe now, when you pass those Buddha images in the shops, you'll have a much better understanding of what they're all about. One of the problems in the West is that Buddhism has too often become mixed up with all sorts of New Age strangeness. There's nothing necessarily wrong with that – after all, Buddhists have been mixing the faith into local cultures since it began – but then it's sometimes hard to tell what is Buddhist belief and what isn't. You should now be able to separate out genuine Buddhist belief from other beliefs which have hitched a ride along with Buddhism. Now you know about Buddhist beliefs you'll also be in a good position to evaluate them too.

The Buddha, Buddhism and Buddhists

Like all religions, there's sometimes a gap between what the original founder taught and what has developed since. The Buddha might be pleased with the way some Buddhists have adapted his teachings, but perhaps not with the way other Buddhists have. The Buddha can't complain though – he did specifically tell people to try it all out for themselves. However, you'll probably find that how Buddhism is expressed by particular Buddhists doesn't always match exactly with what you've learned in this book. Some Buddhists won't accept everything that's written in this book, while others might think learning Buddhism with your brain isn't the point.

You should now have a good grasp of the basics of Buddhism which you can follow up according to your own interests, wherever that might take you. Hopefully you've been given a toolkit to help you work through the claims of the Buddhist faith and also put your own beliefs, or lack of them, to the test. Or maybe you're just content with meditating in that school dining hall ... in which case, the Buddha would be quite happy.

Learning outcomes

There are slight differences between Intermediate 1, 2 and Higher. Make sure your teacher has the latest arrangements documents from the SQA or check them yourself at *www.sqa.org.uk*. To help you, the differences in wording for the World Religions Unit have been put in bold below.

Intermediate 1

1 Demonstrate knowledge and understanding of religious beliefs.

2 Explain the way in which sacred writings, symbols and practices relate to religious beliefs.

3 Express reasoned opinions about the influence of religious beliefs on the lives of members of religious communities.

Intermediate 2

1 Demonstrate knowledge and understanding of religious beliefs.

2 **Explain religious beliefs by examining sources**.

3 **Justify conclusions** about the influence of religious beliefs on the lives of members of religious communities.

Higher

1 Demonstrate knowledge and understanding of religious beliefs.

2 **Analyse** religious beliefs by examining sources.

3 **Evaluate** the influence of religious beliefs on the lives of members of religious communities.

Breadth, Length, Depth

The differentiating factor between Intermediate 1, 2 and Higher can probably be summed up in these three words: breadth, length and depth. The further away from Intermediate 1 you get, the less descriptive you get and the more analytical you're meant to become. This means that you'll probably go into more *depth* in a topic the closer you get to Higher – analysing the whole thing just a little bit more fully and a little bit deeper. You'll also be expected to show more knowledge and understanding the closer you get to Higher. At Intermediate 1 you may take into account one Buddhist viewpoint; at Higher it's likely that you'll take a range of different viewpoints into account. This could be thought of as *breadth*. Finally, you should probably just know more at Higher than at Intermediate 1. You should be able to cover more areas of study and have a wider understanding of those areas – this could be thought of as *length*.

The split of marks in the Unit Assessments (NABs to you) reflects this idea as follows:

NABs marks	Knowledge and Understanding	Analysis and Evaluation
Intermediate 1	70%	30%
Intermediate 2	60%	40%
Higher	60%	40%

In the **final exam**, the split is like this:

Final exam marks	Knowledge and Understanding	Analysis and Evaluation
Intermediate 1	60%	40%
Intermediate 2	50%	50%
Higher	50%	50%

By the time you've read this book, there should be a few past papers for you to look at. Your teacher will have a Specimen Exam Paper from the SQA. This will help them to make up the prelim and give you an idea of what the actual exam might be like. You should also look at the SQA website to find the past exam papers with the marking instructions that the markers use. There's also a new SQA standards website which you (and your teacher) might find helpful.

Sample Assessment Questions (with sample answers)

Here are three sample assessment questions with three sample marking schemes. These are in note-form to give you an idea of the kind of thing which should be included in a good answer. In the exam you should write your answers in prose, but doing a note-form plan is always a good idea, as it saves you wandering off the point. Remember that how clearly you express yourself *does* matter. The NAB questions aren't significantly different from the exam questions in style so we can use these for practice for both. Remember that your NABs are also practice for the final exam!

Intermediate 1

Reminder: There are no prescribed sources at **Intermediate 1**, but there might be stimulus texts in the exam question as below.

Question 1 – The Human Condition

Instructions: *Read the following source then answer all parts of Question 1 (a)–(e). The number of marks available for each part is indicated. Use these as a guide to the amount of detail you should include in your answer.*

> "
> It is the everlasting and unchanging rule of this world that everything is caused by a series of causes and conditions and everything disappears by the same rule; everything changes, nothing remains constant.
>
> *The Teaching of Buddha, by Bukkyo Dendo Kyokai.*

(a) What is Samsara? *(2KU)*

(b) What three creatures are shown in the centre of the wheel of Samsara? *(3KU)*

(c) What is the First Noble Truth? *(1KU)*

(d) 'You can't escape the wheel of life.' Would a Buddhist agree? Give **two** reasons for your answer. *(4AE)*

(Total 10 marks)

Sample Answer

(a)

◆ The wheel of life.

◆ The endless cycle of birth and rebirth.

(a)

◆ Pig.

◆ Cock.

◆ Snake.

(c)

◆ All life is suffering (Dukkha).

(d)

Unusually for an AE answer, there is no 'opposite' for this answer because Buddhists do believe that you can escape the wheel of life – but this just reminds you that an AE answer does not always have to have two sides!

◆ You can escape the wheel of life by attaining Nibbana – this is becoming Enlightened and realising that all things are impermanent.

◆ Throughout successive lives you can build up good Kamma which results in better rebirths, eventually leading to a rebirth where you are in a position to attain Nibbana.

NB Your answer could also mention the role of Arhats and Bodhisattvas.

THE MEANS

Intermediate 2

Question 1 – The Goals

Instructions: *Read the following source then answer all parts of Question 1 (a)–(f). The number of marks available for each part is indicated. Use these as a guide to the amount of detail you should include in your answer.*

> 66
> There is no suffering for him who has finished his journey, and abandoned grief, who has freed himself on all sides, and thrown off all fetters.
>
> *Dhammapada 90*

(a) What are 'fetters'? *(1KU)*

(b) State two examples of fetters in our lives today. *(2KU)*

(c) What do Buddhists understand by Nibbana? *(6KU)*

(d) Explain how Nibbana is linked to kamma. *(5AE)*

(e) Describe how Theravada and Mahayana Buddhists differ in their views about attaining Nibbana. *(6KU)*

(f) 'Nibbana can't be described.' Would a Buddhist agree? *(10AE)*

(Total 30 marks)

Sample Answer

(a)

◆ Anything which ties you to life or holds you down – something which keeps you tied to the wheel of Samsara.

(b)

◆ Anything which you might 'cling on to' in life which keeps you from recognising that everything is impermanent.

◆ So fetters could be material things of any kind or concepts like fame, popularity, desire, etc.

(c)

◆ Enlightenment.

◆ The realisation that all things are impermanent and so being freed from this illusion.

◆ Understanding the way things are.

◆ Escaping the endless cycles of birth and rebirth by no longer being reborn and so escaping suffering.

◆ Understanding the true nature of Reality.

◆ Becoming one with Reality.

◆ Removing the fuel for the flames of rebirth.

Answer might make reference to the Enlightenment of the Buddha as a model.

(d)

◆ Kamma is both the consequences of our actions and the actions themselves.

◆ Aim is to develop good Kamma and not bad Kamma.

◆ Kamma is linked to rebirth and Samsaric cycle.

◆ Must gain good Kamma to have a rebirth where Enlightenment becomes a possibility.

◆ May make reference to the Three Root Poisons and their relationship to the gaining of good Kamma.

Skilful actions might also be discussed and how these help the individual progress towards Nibbana.

(e)

Theravada:

◆ Description and explanation of the Arhat and various stages of becoming one – for example, stream entrant, etc.

◆ Mention elements involved in becoming an Arhat – for example, Sila, Samadhi, Panna.

◆ Likelihood of becoming an Arhat is greater if you are part of the monastic community.

Mahayana:

◆ Description and explanation of the Bodhisattva and how to become one – various stages of Bodhisattvahood, for example, Bodhicitta, Dhyana, Prajna, etc.

◆ Possible focus on the concepts of Prajna and Karuna, and Bodhisattva's well-developed abilities in relation to skilful actions.

(f)

Agree:

◆ Can only be experienced.

◆ Cannot communicate the experience to someone who has not shared it – there's no common point of reference.

◆ Is a state of mind rather than a place.

◆ Can explain more easily what it is not than what it is.

◆ Can be attained during life but once attained the one who has attained it is not likely to boast about it.

◆ May focus on the word 'described' – how easy is it to describe something which isn't really anything?

Disagree:

◆ Is removing the fuel for the flames of rebirth – so can communicate that idea of freeing yourself from the fetters which hold you back from Enlightenment.

◆ Can use the Buddha's Enlightenment as a model for explanation.

◆ Can say what it is not.

◆ Is becoming aware of the impermanence of all things and of the true nature of Reality – this is an explanation.

◆ If you cannot explain it, how would you know when you had attained it?

◆ If Arhats and Bodhisattvas attain it and then help others to do so too, then there must be something meaningful they can convey to others about what it is.

Higher

Question 1 – The Means

Instructions: *Read the following source then answer **all** parts of Question 1 (a)–(f). The number of marks available for each part is indicated. Use these as a guide to the amount of detail you should include in your answer.*

> Cut down the whole forest (of lust), not a tree only! Danger comes out of the forest (of lust). When you have cut down both the forest (of lust) and its undergrowth, then, Bhikkhus, you will be rid of the forest and free!
>
> — *Dhammapada 283*

(a) Which of the Five Precepts is this source most likely to be referring to? *(1KU)*

(b) In what different ways might Buddhists observe this Precept? *(6KU)*

(c) Explain what Buddhists understand by the Precept, 'Do not distort facts'. *(4KU)*

(d) Why might it be difficult for a modern Buddhist to follow the Precept, 'Do not distort facts'? *(6AE)*

(e) How does the Threefold Way help Buddhists progress towards Enlightenment? *(4KU, 4AE)*

(f) 'All the rules and requirements of Buddhism are simply the application of compassion.' Would a Buddhist agree? *(5AE)*

(Total 30 marks)

Sample Answer

(a)

◆ Refrain from the misuse of the senses.

(or expressed positively as)

◆ Cultivate responsibility for the feelings of others.

(b)

Lay people:

◆ Would mean responsibility within a sexual relationship – being faithful to your partner or being considerate towards the person with whom you're having the relationship.

◆ Not benefiting in any way from the exploitation of another person's emotions.

◆ Controlling the emotions in relation to sexual behaviour so as to stay on the path to Enlightenment.

◆ Being sensible about the amount of sensory stimulation of all kinds that we expose ourselves to.

Monks/Nuns:

◆ Most likely to mean that they will abstain from sex altogether.

Also means that monks and nuns will try to detach themselves from worldly pleasures – so could describe some of the practical examples of this, for example, not using high chairs or having comfortable beds.

(c)

◆ Telling direct lies.

◆ Telling lies indirectly by omitting to tell the truth or telling the truth in such a way which distorts the reality.

◆ Exaggerating the truth.

◆ Gossiping and using speech as a way of creating your own reality rather than what is truly real.

(d)

◆ Advertising often makes claims about products which could be examples of exaggeration (or even outright lies)

◆ 'Selling ourselves' at job interviews and the like might mean that we expand the truth somewhat; our very competitive world might mean that we end up exaggerating and expanding the truth so as to create or maintain advantages over others.

◆ Newspapers and TV tend to sensationalise things and present a slightly distorted image of what is real – it's hard to escape this.

(e)

Threefold Way should be explained and link to Nibbana made:

◆ Wisdom – finding out the truth of the Dhamma for yourself: this leads to you removing ignorance and becoming less attached to things. This detachment leads towards Enlightenment. Link to the idea that learning the Dhamma is about learning to experience it rather than just learning it mentally – in the same way, Enlightenment cannot be explained, only experienced.

◆ Morality – acting upon your understanding by living in the right way. This will reflect your awareness of the true nature of Reality. Should also discuss the ideas of skilful and unskilful actions – changing your moral behaviour in relation to the person or the situation.

◆ Meditation – seeing things as they really are. You cannot become Enlightened until you have reflected on how things truly are and come to understand that and what it means for your beliefs and practice.

(f)

Yes:

◆ Compassion for all beings is expressed in loving kindness and the application of skilful actions in your moral choices.

◆ The specific rules can all be reduced to the principle of being mindful of others and yourself.

◆ What you do in life – from sexual behaviour to the height of your chair – is related to what you think life's goals are. In Buddhism, you are aiming to become detached from the illusion of Reality and make progress towards Enlightenment. You are far more likely to do the 'little' right things if the big right thing (compassion) is already in place.

No:

◆ It is unlikely that a Buddhist would argue against compassion being a key feature in Buddhist thinking and ethical life; however, you could point out that compassion could be a vague and not very specific thing to follow in life if it wasn't backed up by very practical things like doing a caring job.

◆ People need specifics to show them what the principle of compassion means in everyday life.

Final words

Your teacher will go over exam technique until you're really quite sick of it so let's not do that here. Just remember that, specific to this course, you're really being expected to show the following things:

◆ That you have a knowledge and understanding of Buddhist beliefs.

◆ That you can back this up using relevant Buddhist sources where appropriate.

◆ That you know and can discuss how all of this affects Buddhists as individuals and in groups in everyday life.

Remember that you have been learning about what Buddhists believe and do. You might be asked to express your own view on that in an assessment. You might not. Just make sure you know when to and when not to – and if you do, always do so in a reasonable way showing that you have benefited from a year's study of the topic!

Also, remember that when the exam is over you don't have to forget it all when you hand this book back to your teacher (very bad kamma if you forget this). Learning should go on throughout your whole life. Buddhism, like all religions (and so RMPS), is about humanity's search for meaning, value and purpose in life. One name for Buddhism is the way of the Buddha (Buddha Vinaya), but the Buddha encouraged us to find our own way. May you find your way.

THE MEANS

Index

Page numbers in italics indicate illustrations.